Selfhood as Thinking Thought in the Work of Gabriel Marcel:
A New Interpretation

by

Francisco L. Peccorini

Problems in Contemporary Philosophy
Volume 3

The Edwin Mellen Press
Lewiston/Queenston

Library of Congress Cataloging-in-Publication Data

Peccorini, Francisco L.
  Selfhood as thinking thought in the work of Gabriel Marcel.

  (Problems in contemporary philosophy ; v. 3)
  Bibliography: p.
  Includes index.
  1. Marcel, Gabriel, 1889-1973. 2. Self (Philosophy)--
History--20th century. I. Title. II. Series.
B2430.M254P43 1987   126'.092'4   86-28549
ISBN 0-88946-329-8

This is volume 3 in the continuing series
Problems in Contemporary Philosophy
Volume 3 ISBN 0-88946-329-8
PCP Series ISBN 0-88946-325-5

Printed in the United States of America

To Tita, my wife
whose "Marcellian Communion" was
so instrumental in this research.

Table of Contents

Acknowledgments

I want to express my sincere gratitude in the first place to the Institute for the Encyclopedia of Ultimate Reality and Meaning, and in particular, to its General Editor, Professor Tibor Horvath, and to Professor Stanley Grean (Ohio University, Athens), who is in charge of the Philosophy Section, for the constant and encouraging support they gave to my project. Let my gratitude go , in the second place, to Professor Grace Natoli (St. John's University, Jamaica, N.Y.), whose enlightening response to my paper was so great an asset in my further investigation.

Introduction
A "Follow-up" to a Past Research

A "caveat lector" is in order from the very outset of this introduction.

Indeed, the reader should not expect a methodical and exhaustive expose of Marcel's philosophy. Other books, written in that vein, are available; and I myself wrote one in 1959 [Gabriel Marcel: La "Razón de Ser" en la "Participación" (Barcelona: Editorial Juan Flors, 1959)], in which I pursued some of the typically Marcellian issues that I purposefully overlooked in this more specialized research that I am now presenting.

In particular, there I lavishly elaborated on topics such as the crack pointed to by Marcel in the process of knowledge, which resulted in his famous binomial "knowledge by participation versus objective knowledge," as well as in the "it-thou" opposition, the enlightening distinction "Truth (or spirit of truth) vs. truths," the antithetic approaches to the "problematic," on the one hand, and to the mysterious "metaproblematic," on the other, and finally the differences in depth of activities such as thinking and thinking at (penser, penser à), which go straight to support the core of Marcel's "concrete" philosophy. Most of all, though, I tackled the nature of the basic "existential judgment;" and one might even say that if any merit is to be found in that work, it is that it traces down to Marcel's historical entry of December 3, 1920, in his Metaphysical Journal, what constitutes Marcel's own liberation from those agonizing misgivings about the existential judgment that he had been enduring for so long on the grounds of such a judgment's apparent "objectivity" (see o.c., pp. 283-315, mainly pp. 304-315). It is then that Marcel discovered the first pole of his brand of Existentialism, namely, the "participation in Existence." Given the extreme importance of that basic Marcellian landmark, perhaps it would be advisable to insert here a short parenthesis to brief the reader on my findings before we start our present study on the second pole of this philosophy, the "participation in Being," which is required to cover the whole Marcellian trajectory as outlined by Troisfontaines in the title of his famous commentary, De l'Existence à l'Être.

In his attempt to reduce all certainty about existence to his basic and irrefutable experience-limit, which is no other than the Urgefühl or the feeling of his body inasmuch as it is "his," in January 1920 Marcel came to conceive of the existential judgment in function of such an experience. Unfortunately, he did it in such a way that he confined himself to "conceptualizing" the very Urgefühl itself. As he put it at that time, he came to understand that "Reflective thought thus posits the judgment of existence as being the transposition of the experience-limit into the intellectual order (where there are objects and judgments bearing on those objects); and this goes for any judgment of existence whatever. From this standpoint we can see how only that which is capable of entering into relations of contact, i.e. spatial relations with my body, can be said to exist. That may serve as a definition" (MJ, p. 25). Yet, he could not be happy with his understanding of

existence as a relation, namely, as the spatial relation
of an object to my body, which hints of a real concept
and is, by the same token, universal in essence. The
idea that there was something wrong with that approach
became a burden for him during the whole year of 1920,
until finally on December 3, he detected in that
description a hidden detail that had by force to wrest
existence from the realm of the universals. Already on
November the 18th of the same year he had come to
realize that if in the very process of forming a notion
a personal element happened to appear as built into that
notion, such a grasp could in no way be of a real
object. That criterion was indubitable to him precisely
because he had already reached the conclusion that "it
is essential to the very nature of the object not to
take `me' into account" (MJ, p. 261). This led him to
deny that his notion of God could be a concept proper.
He wrote: "this impersonal thought which is the only
foundation for objects cannot be constituted other than
on the basis of personal consciousness. The inexpress-
ible quality of immediate experience vanished in the
course of the dialectic by which the object is constituted" (MJ, p. 261). But by the same token he could
understand that the aforementioned notion of existence
Could not be a concept either--and this precisely to the
extent that it cannot form part of any real dialectic
process. "An idea occurred to me this afternoon"-- he
wrote on the third of December--"that may be important.
could we not say that any judgment of existence implies
a deviation of the mind from the dialectical attitude
that makes the affirmation of any object possible?" (MJ,
pp. 268-269). Evidently that deviation could only be
caused by the fact that a personal element, namely the
reference to my body precisely as mine, was necessarily

built into the notion of "existence." This allowed him finally to conclude: "Long ago I realised that every existant must appear to me as prolonging my body in some direction -- my body inasmuch as it is mine, that is to say, inasmuch as it is non-objective" (MJ, p. 269). And this meant that the notion of existence could not be a concept proper precisely because it is the natural expression of man's incarnation. "The world exists"--he added--"in the measure in which I have relations with it--which are of the same type as my relations with my own body" (ibid.).

It is well known how important that discovery was for Marcel. It opened, in fact, the door of his peculiar type of existentialism, thereby letting him leave behind for ever the smothering walls of Brunschwicg's idealism that had been literally suffocating his soul for so many years. Yet, important as it is within Marcel's entire doctrinal body, I did not include it in this book; furthermore, if I summarized in this introduction the abundant treatment that I had reserved for it in 1959, it was only in order better to setthe stage on which the Marcel of the Pensée pensante, who is the real concern of this new work, could stand up and show us his true face. In turn, the reason for this new approach was the need to answer a very definite question that was laid down for discussion during the second biennial meeting of the Institute for the Encyclopedia of Ultimate Reality and Meaning held in Toronto at the end of August, 1983; a question that I had committed myself to answer.

Indeed, having to propose an ultimate reality and meaning for Marcel's approach to human existence, i.e.

having to single out the determining insight that, according to the philosopher, accounts for the totality of aspects of man's Being, and in particular for the blinded intuition as well as for faith, freedom, hope, the ontological appetite, love, recollection, intersubjectivity, and the moral law's attraction, I zeroed in on his conception of the pensée pensante in its capacity as the constitution of the unverifiable self. My summarized solution came out in the Journal of the same organization in its first issue of 1985, under the title "Gabriel Marcel's Pensée Pensante as the Ultimate Reality and Meaning," [see URAM, 8 (1985), n.1.]. But by then, as announced in the presentation of the issue by Prof. Tibur Horvath, General Editor of URAM, I was already working on this book, which constitutes an elaboration on what I presented to the audience in 1983.

The peculiar aspect of this new work will stand out if we compare the interests that presided over the two approaches. We might say in that connection that--to use Marcel's own philosophical language-- in 1959 I focused on a case of Marcellian "problematic" phenomenology--a case of deep and attentive concentration on our personal experience.., whereas in 1985 I am being led to single out cases of what we might call "metaproblematic" phenomenology, the kind of phenomenology that cannot be carried out without a second reflection. Indeed, the scope of this study encompasses both the most fundamental issue, which is the constitution of the pure subject, and some of the existential phenomena such as the blinded intuition, faith, hope, fidelity, and love, into which the unverifiable pure subject blooms out. Furthermore, since the aforementioned "Experience-limit" itself, as well as the distinctions that we mentioned at the outset as objects of my 1959 concern, are but direct manifestations of the nature of the thinking-thought, we might add that the present research goes after the roots of those Marcellian landmarks.

The just-mentioned methodological distinction, "problematic phenomenology vs. metaproblematic phenomenology," does clearly call for some comment. Seymour Cain rightly pointed out that Marcel has a peculiar kind of phenomenology. Comparing it with Husserl's version, he wrote: "Broadly speaking, then, Marcel's method is phenomenological, but there are basic contrasts between his metaphysical position and that of Husserl. As with his existential thought, Marcel worked out his phenomenological approach on his own hook, at his own pace, in his own particular way; if this is phenomenology, it is Marcellian rather than Husserlian" [See Seymour Cain, Gabriel Marcel (South Bend, Indiana: Regency/Gateway, 1963), pp. 99]. As much as it is refreshing to see Marcel recognized as a uniquely personal full-fledged phenomenologist, it is disappointing to realize that Cain did not break the much-pondered difference down to its particulars after so much ado about it. In an effort to make up for such an omission, I surmise that the abovementioned contrast consists, on the one hand, in the object that concerned both philosophers--a problematic reality in the case of Husserl, and a metaproblematical one in the concrete Marcellian philosophy--, and, on the other hand, in the distinct methods that both of them followed-- the primary reflection, which lingers on the object's essence, in Husserl's type of phenomenology, and the second reflection, which inquires into the phenomenon's ultimate conditions of possibility, as Marcel does most of the time. However, he too can occasionally exercise the problematic kind of phenomenology, as he showed so well in connection with the Urgefühl in the Metaphysical Journal. The second reflection type of phenomenology that Marcel introduced on his own would seem to bear out the claim that he once expressed to the effect that he was interested in phenomenology only to the extent that it serves as a platform from which to launch his metaphysical research. Indeed, the infinitely fecund ontological nature of the pensée pensante, for one, fully warrants many far-reaching existential consequences once it has been put on display phenomenologically.

Among the metaphysical inquiries that I have focused upon in the present work by using the pensée pensante as a springboard, I should mention Marcel's contention that human nature alone, without the support of revealed data, is enough to build up a sublime and heart-lifting type of Ethics, which holds steadfast onto the claims of a concrete philosophy. The last chapter bears it out, and so also does chapter IV, where Christ's light is brought down to the mere philosophical level and made to bear on the foundation of the Community. Cain, who is willing to recognize this achievement, seems to surmise that Marcel is herein emphasizing an absolute dichotomy between concrete philosophy and abstract thought. He objects to Marcel's claims the the achievements of the classical philosophers, who, in his view, succeeded in combining abstract with concrete elements:

> Can abstract thought too be the
> medium, the form of expression, of
> an existentially rooted drive toward

ontological participation? Is not
something like this the basic
intention of the great philosophers
of the past--of an Aristotle and
Aquinas, and also of a Plato and a
Descartes? Can what Marcel calls
`the whole being' be committed and
involved in the life-vocation of
abstract thought?
(O.c., p. 118)

My position is diametrically opposed to Cain's
fears. In the last chapter I make it clear that Marcel
advocates a concrete approach to Morality, in which the
particular circumstances have much to say through the
individual's conscience, without thereby having to
neglect the guiding force of the essence qua nature,
which is a powerful pointer that encourages us to
imitate God's perfection. In other words, he is only
against the type of ethical rationalism introduced by
Grotius and Puffendorf, who built a whole moral system
on pure reason without even looking once at experience
to take from it some cues. As for the Classics, far
from accusing St. Thomas of such an extreme rationalism,
Marcel openly attributed to Christian philosophy and
Theology the status of role-model for the XXth century
moralists. "They deserve the undying glory," - he wrote
- "not only for not having ignored it [the right combination of the universal demands of human nature and the
requirements of a concrete situation, carried out in the
light of Being], but also for having brought it up,
instead, to its zenith and grounded it in the inde-
structible foundations of Being" (Homo Viator, French
edition, p. 34). As far as Aristotle's philosophy is

concerned, 'he made it a point to recognize that his own
thought was essentially Aristotelian, as he confessed to
Pierre Boutang when the latter inquired whether
Aristotle's theory of the agent intellect had anything
to do with his emphasis on the light of Christ. And we
might add that even Marcel's stand on the distinction
between the body/object and the body/self, as Cain puts
it (see O.C., pp. 117-118), is pure Aristotelian stuff
despite the impressive objection raised against it by
Cain himself to the effect that one cannot see the
relation between the one and the other. It is
Aristotelian because it simply comes down to considering
the body respectively from without, first, and then as
the conscious existence of the self in the world, which
is the same as the human experience insofar as it encompasses also the "informing" activity of the sensible
power of the soul on matter in the latter's capacity as
a potential human body. But we all know very well that
to call it "Aristotelian" is not the same as to declare
it "conceptually intelligible." Aristotle himself was
led to realize this distinction the hard way. Indeed,
in his De Anima, as we all know, he was forced to
grapple very often with realities that stubbornly kept
slipping away from his naturalistic and scientific
tendencies. Marcel, too, experienced the same problem
in connection with his body "as his own," which certainly belongs to the metaproblematic realm. Indeed, he
tried a rational explanation, as we already saw--he
wrote: "But if this is so my body is only felt inasmuch
as it is m e-as-acting: feeling is a function of acting"
(MJ, p. 260)--, but he gave it up in a bout of insatis-
faction, settling rather for something less explanatory:
"Thus" --he added-- "I believe that the formula can only
be given a negative meaning: i.e. it is not true to say

that I am not my body, that my body is exterior to a certain central reality of myself, for no truth regarding the relation binding this pseudo-reality with my body is possible." (ibid).

The character of "unverifiability" had to impose itself, therefore, on Marcel's search for the ultimate reality and meaning of human existence. This warrants fully the title of the present book: Selfhood as Thinking Thought in the Work of Gabriel Marcel: A New Interpretation.

Francisco L. Peccorini

California State University,
Long Beach.

Chapter I

A Growing Thought Becomes Life

Who was Gabriel Marcel? Considering the long and active career of the biographee and the intrinsic difficulty pointed out by Marcel himself, this question is practically "unanswerable." "My life"--he wrote in the last attempt on his part at bequeathing his memoirs to us--"Cannot be presented in filing cards; that is what I mean when I say that a life cannot be told."[1] On the other hand, since his philosophy is but his inner experience lifted to the level of thought, it behooves the rest of this book to let the real Marcel introduce himself with the fullness of his spiritual life.

He was born December 7, 1889, in the typically Parisian Monceaux plaine quartier, but his childhood was not altogether uncloudy since his mother's early death was already lurking in the near future. From our point of view his premature orphanage was decisive since it was bound to leave in his mind a lasting and definitive orientation. His father--who functioned at different times as "Conseiller d'État," plenipotentiary minister of France in Stockholm and Fine Arts director-- did what he could to make up for Gabriel's education, which he entrusted to his sister-in-law whom he later married.

Marcel attended the Carnot Lyceum and the Sorbonne, and it was in the latter that, upon the defense of a thesis on Coleridge's metaphysical ideas in relation to Schelling's philosophy, he obtained in 1907 his "diplôme d'études supérieures," and it was there too that in 1910 he was granted the "Agrégation de philosophie."

His early professional activities were devoted to secondary education: Vendôme 1912, Paris 1915-1918, Sens 1919-1922; and so were a few years before his official entrance to the "hall of fame":Paris 1939-40, Montpellier 1941. In between he worked as a reader for several publishers--this opportunity enabled him to create the series called "Feux Croisés," which was called upon to introduce to the French public foreign writers such as Aldous Huxley and Ernst Junger--and he contributed many literary articles to Europe Nouvelle, Nouvelle Revue Française, and other well-known journals. Even during his philosophical career he doubled as a journalist through the dramatic criticisms that he wrote for Nouvelles Littéraires from 1945 to 1968.

He received all kinds of honors, among which he was very fond of the honoris causa doctorates that he received from several outstanding Universities, among which the Universities of Tokyo, Chicago, and Salamanca are worth mentioning. In 1949 he was granted the Grand Prix of Literature by the Académie Française, and in 1952 the Académie de Sciences morales et politiques made him one of its members. He also cherished the "Prix Erasme"--which he shared with the physicist Carl Friedrich von Weizsacker in Rotterdam on the 27th. On October of 1969 it was delivered to him by Prince Berhard in the presence of Queen Juliana--and the "Prix

de la Paix," which was handed down to him by Heinrich
Lubke, president of West Germany, on behalf of the
German Booksellers in September 1964 at Frankfurt.

Marcel died in Paris on the 8th of October of 1973.

His life was devoted to philosophy, which he understood as reflection on experience. In this sense he
became involved in telepathic paraphenomena and even
acted as a medium in certain spiritualistic seances. It
should be added, though, that he always took those
experiences as springboards for his philosophical pur-
suits, and only when he had become quite sure that no
other account could be found for them except a real
spiritual communication.2

And it is precisely this involvement with
experience--with concrete philosophy, we should say--
that finally prevailed in the eyes of the public, which
up to the forties had ranked him among the contemporary
catholic philosophers, a kind of Neo-Thomist of sorts.
From the forties on he began to be considered as the
depositary of a new kind of thought which was finally
identified with Existentialism, a characterization that
both he and Heidegger rejected on the grounds that it
had become ambiguous after having been unduly appropriated by Jean Paul Sartre.

The following classification might be closer to the
truth, perhaps. Marcel's thought--which spread rapidly
through multilingual translations and through his own
living messages brought in person through his lectures
to the whole world--presents many facets: he was a
challenging playwright, a deep metaphysician--mainly in

view in his early writings--, a phenomenologist, and
what some have come to call an existentialist thinker
but does in fact amount to what we might call a
philosopher of hope and communion--in one word, the
philosopher with a young thought that appeals to young
generations because it addresses the anxieties of young
people in the face of the threats that technology wields
against the survival of our world. It is this last
characteristic that insured him a Hollywood-type
success in the United States.

The warm welcome he received at Gonzaga University
in Spokane is a case in point. Michael Moffit describes
in America[3] the excitement that the announcement of his
visit had aroused among the students and faculty and the
unexpected way in which it was exceeded by an overflow-
ing crowd that literally took over the campus and came
even from the non-student population. At 7:30, he adds,
"there were 200 people in the foyer and several hundred
more making their way toward the auditorium." The
gathering audience had to be transferred to the Student
Union. "In a few minutes they had filled the 900 chairs
hurriedly set up in the hall. Another 400 people sat on
window sills, on the floor around the speaker's platform
and on tables at the far end of the hall."[4] To quote
once again the same article: "A conservative estimate
put the total, including those who were discouraged and
went home, at about sixteen hundred." Useless to mention that there was a thunderous ovation at the end, and
that Marcel was deeply moved by it.

This was not a passing phenomenon. Speaking of his
several trips to America, mainly in 1959 and 1966, he
could write in his memoirs: "I do not think that it was

pure chance that my thought spread in the United States faster than in certain European countries, mainly after the lectures that I was invited to deliver at Harvard during the Fall semester of 1961."[5] And we should not forget that those William James lectures had the usual appeal for the young since they bore precisely on the existential background of human existence. It goes without saying that his success concerned only the young people, for he adds in his memoirs that "his meetings with the Professors at Harvard, who are all neo-positivists except for a few ones, were merely formal and a matter of courtesy."[56] "But during some seminars that I gave in addition to my lectures," he goes on to point out, "I established a real rapport with a certain number of students, an experience that I renewed in different universities, mainly at Cleveland, Pittsburgh, San Francisco, etc."[7] Somewhere else he recognized that the same enthusiasm could be found among his young Japanese audiences--and even among his Indian readers-- due undoubtedly to the oriental flavor of his thought. This is why, after mentioning that his works had been translated in their entirety into the Japanase language, he adds: "I learned also that mainly in Kyoto some students had been lastingly impressed--as it seemed--by the insights on immortality that I had conveyed to them."[8]

In Professor Vincent Berning's view, his thought had not yet had a visible success in Germany because as an existential thinker Marcel had to compete with Heidegger's philosophy which monopolized the German intellectual establishment for years, and as a philosopher of the "Thou" his place had been preempted by Martin Buber, with whom he had to share the audiences and the readers, and whose linguistic advantage was unbeatable. It was only in the Catholic milieux that he always found a favorable echo, even recently among thinkers such as John B. Lotz and Karl Rahner due to the new approach that Joseph Marechal, who had turned Thomism into a kind of transcendental philosophy, had made popular among them. And it was only when the French began to be interested in Marcel as a phenomenogist--questionable as this label may be-- that the Germans followed suit. One of the most authoritative phenomenological manuals in Germany today, John Hering's The Phenomenological Movement, in a very detailed and important study dubs Marcel a French phenomenologist. Professor Berning sees also a renewal brewing in some quarters through the work written by C.F. Bollnow and Klaus Schaller, Histoire de l'education et de la culture, which draws heavily on Marcel's concepts of incarnation, disposability and communion, but most of all through his appeal to the young generations. He states: "in my capacity as a professor who is in touch with the students, I know that this thought is young and therefore has a future also in Germany."9

Indeed, his thought, which is worth considering, will keep on calling on the minds because the International Association, "Présence de Gabriel Marcel," which was created in 1975 with the help of the "Fondation Européenne de la Culture," will certainly see to it that the smoldering flame of his message never dies. Together with Michaele Federico Sciacca's philosophy of integrality, Marcel's philosophy of hope, which roots all our potentials in our direct participation in Being, would certainly be the answer to the anxieties aroused by the threat of an atomic holocaust in the hearts of the youngsters.

And yet, so existentially engaging an approach to reality may not be, after all, but the old Thomist thought soaked in our current tragic experience and updated so that it may measure up to the needs of the twentieth-century man. Indeed, as I myself tried to show in my book, Gabriel Marcel: "La Razón de Ser" en la "Participación," on the occasion of describing Marcel's early gropings in search of an Ontology through what he then used to call a positive dialectic and later on came to designate as primary reflection, the grounds for the identification offered up to the forties are not altogether negligible. In that book I had the privilege of being granted permission to use some manuscripts which at that time were still unpublished and portions of which I translated into Spanish while referring to them in accordance with Roger Troisfontaines's classical classification.10 For this reason, herein I will confine myself to outlining that first period of his thought, a detailed exposé of which can also be found in my article, "The Ontological Route in the Light of Marcel and Sciacca," which was published by Sciacca himself in his own Giornale di Metafisica.11

In those unpublished manuscripts Marcel was desperately trying to untangle himself from the snares and the tight grip of the kind of Idealism that he had been forced to inherit from his illustrious mentor, Léon Brunschvicg, by forcefully struggling with the negation "Being is not." In Manuscript XXII, for instance, he came to the conclusion that such a negation was impossible, not precisely because it might be considered contradictory by some readers, but because it is meaningless since it is impossible to use it in a totally univocal sense. But precisely his realization that the notion of being ("that which is") is not univocal but rather analogical was about to fling him into the greatest discovery of his lifetime, to which he would come _via_ logical discourse alone, through the analysis of the content of our foremost concept. Indeed, such an insight, in which Being shows up in many different ways, necessarily leads to the impression of being involved in an infinite transcendent and all-encompassing reality that he finally called the Concrete Universal. At the time, though, he could not find any better philosophical support for it than Bergson's thought, which permitted him to draw the line between Being, as the hidden concrete universal source of all beings, and the latter as the appearances of the former. In fact, though,he had reached what St. Thomas Aquinas called _esse_ and _actus_ _essendi_. Unfortunately then he did not know what to do with it. On the one hand, he had only the _primary_ _reflection_ or conceptual approach available, and such an approach, which works only on the question, "what is it?", had already proven insufficient for any research that must go beyond the phenomenal world; whereas, on the other hand, the _blind_ _intuition_, which later on would put him in touch with Being-in-itself, had not yet been retrieved because Marcel had not yet come across the magic _second_ _reflection_, which would be based on the examination of the condition of possibility of any "given."

A masterful discussion in his Gifford Lectures showed the impossibility of conceptualizing Being-in-itself.[12] As a result, the kind of negative stand or second reflection was going to remain for ever his "Ontology," if we are allowed to use the term in this connection. He went over it in 1968 during the kind of seminar that was published under the title of <u>Pour</u> <u>une</u> <u>sagesse</u> <u>tragique</u>.

We might say that at that time he had finally reached the "unverifiable" on which his whole thought was going to rest. He showed therein that, unlike the question, "What is it to be passive?"--which still makes sense because it refers to a certain aspect, unverifiable as it may be, of a subject which can really be thought of as a being--the question on Being is entirely elusive. "Thus"--he wrote--"the precise form of my question ought to be `What is it for this <u>upokeimenon</u> (I much prefer the Greek word) to act or to be passive?'"[13] And he added: "It seems to me--and here I am radically opposed to Heidegger--that really this question `What is it for this being to be?' cancels itself out...when I was questioning myself about what it was for an acting subject to act, my question bore on what appeared to me as a specifying modality. Correctly or not, I was thinking of the subject as somehow being before it was specified in acting."[14] After all, he was still moving within the primary reflection. But the question of Being did not fit in that reflection at all. The reason is that it was fully unverifiable. Hence, dismissing forever the primary reflection, he concluded: "We must therefore say...that strictly speaking one cannot question being since every question presupposes being as a base."[15] And yet he still had to struggle with the unavoidable recognition of the ontological exigency, which he finally tried to describe as follows: "It seems that it is the impossibility of any confining-within. Perhaps it would be better to say the impossibility of any `reducing to something else;' or more simply and truly, `to something,' for what cannot be `other than' cannot be `this or that' either. Thus we are well into the nonqualifiable."[16]

This is obviously no longer an instantiation of what he formerly had designated as "metaproblematic" during the 1937 International Convention. "No doubt"-- he added--"it would be better to introduce the word `hypo-problematic,' which much better indicates that here we are **beneath** the level where problems have their place."[17]

Evidently, Gabriel Marcel could not be satisfied with those results of a positive dialectic, even though the latter had led him to the discovery of Being as the Being of all things in its capacity as the <u>Concrete Universal</u>. Encouraged by Bergson, though, he was bent upon locating Being intuitively through negative dialectic. It was to be expected, therefore, that the latter would be tried first in the depths of the human spirit, that comes also under the name of "thinking thought."

footnotes

[1]En chemin vers quel éveil? [EChE], p. 15

[2]O.c., pp. 100-110, 220; Entretiens autour de Gabriel Marcel (Neuchâtel, 1976), p. 160.

[3]America (Nov. 30, 1963), pp. 708-709.

[4]Ibid.

[5]EChE, p. 258.

[6]O.c., p. 259.

[7]Ibid.

[8]O.c., p. 281.

[9]See: Entretiens autour de Gabriel Marcel, p. 219. See also: Cheetham, "L'actualité du `Monde Cassé' de G. Marcel," in Revue de Métaphysique et de Morale, 79 (1974), pp. 367-370.

[10]See: Troisfontaines, Roger, De l'Existence à l'Être, 1953 and 1968, Bibliography.

[11]See: Peccorini, F.L., "The Ontological Route in the Light of Marcel and Sciacca", in Giornale de Metafisica, 28 (1973), pp. 481-523, mainly 481-485.

[12]See: Marcel, The Mystery of Being, [MB], II, pp. 21-37, 58-76.

[13]See: Marcel, Tragic Wisdom and Beyond, 1973, [TrW], p. 48.

[14]Ibid.

[15] O.c., p. 49.

[16] O.c., p. 50.

[17] O.c., p. 51.

Chapter II

Being as the Pure Subject: The Root of Existence

Marcel's attempt at locating Being through intuition gives him the opportunity fully to clarify one of his most basic concepts, the concept of "pensée pensante" or <u>thinking thought</u>, which he contrasts with the concept of "pensée pensée" or <u>conceptualized thought</u>."1

1 - <u>The Self as the "Pensée pensante</u>."

As soon as he enters this path, he is literally dragged to face the mystery of self-hood. "In thought"--he writes--"there is something that can in no way whatsoever be an idea and that something is evidently the very kernel of thought itself." He then specifies in what sense he is taking thought within this context. "It is thought insofar as it affirms"--he says--"not insofar as it is affirmed, i.e. not as an idea." And, what is still more important, he goes on to state the reasons that lead him to equate it with Being, and they are such that it is difficult to separate pure thought as understood by the French philosopher from the Aristotelian soul,2 namely, as the self-consciousness of Being itself insofar as it is the infinite root of all possibilities, and this amounts to the soul as acting in its capacity as possible intellect. "Thought taken in that sense"--he points out--"seems to correspond to that which we called Being. At least it is necessary to recognize in it some affinities with Being insofar as it too is different from the idea of Being (different from Absolute Knowledge) and cannot undergo any criterion since to that effect it would have to be transformed first into an idea."[3] The allusion to the Aristotelian blank slate is clear. Yet the Aristotelian flavor will come out more penetrating still as we go ahead in the footsteps of Marcel. But even in his Du Refus à l'Invocation (Creative Fidelity, in English), where he officially introduced the technical term of pensée pensante to the world, his identifying it with the source of our acts of understanding and sensibility--in one word, with our concrete experience of being in the world--strongly reminds us of the original dynamism of the soul that Aristotle tried to describe in his De Anima, III, 5, 430a 10-15, as the purest type of dynamism, a dynamism, in sum, whose purity he rendered through the famous epistemological formula of the blank slate and which allowed him to conceive of the whole process of experience in ontological terms as a process by which the soul progressively comes to share its actuality with the objects of knowledge that it assimilates as they come along. This makes it most enlightening to trace these two Aristotelian aspects of human psychology to the very official explicitation of the concept of pensée pensante in Marcel's Creative Fidelity. For he too clearly roots the soul in Being in such a way that he finds in it the foundations of both co-presence and our sense of universal brotherhood; and, of course, thereby he opens up the infinity of Being in front of our spirit. Being, in turn, acting as a magnet, can then proceed to trigger all our ideals and aspirations. Furthermore, Marcel too calls it "thought," not in the sense that it is a representation, but rather in the sense that all representations are made possible by it. "Such a thought"--he writes, clearly emphasizing its capacity as a power or faculty of research--"is exercised in the search for truth and...is the source of our universal judgments."[4] Indeed, he does not ignore that "a thought which is anchored in experience is not your property or mine, but fortunately exists apart from all these impoverished descriptions which distort it."[5] Of course, in this he is not alone. Yet he interprets this community of thought and experience in a newer and deeper sense. In his view, we all participate in it because ultimately it is nothing but Being asserting its presence in me. As he would put it at the peak of his production--and this shows that Marcel's philosophy never deflected an inch from what he had discovered between the years of 1910 and 1914, as will be seen in a moment[6]--, we are the stage of Being. He recognized "that the whole reflexive process remains within a certain assertion which I am-- rather than I pronounce--an assertion of which I am the place and not the subject."[7]

It is clear, therefore, that through his life-long use of second reflection he had been "led to assume or recognise a form of participation which has the reality of a subject," and that in his view, "this participation cannot be, by definition, an object of thought."[8] We should not lose sight, either, of the fact that this is the same participation to which he resorts within the context of Creative Fidelity to shed light on the meaning of "pensée pensante," which is there intimately associated with existence as the immediate living source of the latter. "Existence," he writes, "or better, existentiality, if I may be allowed to use this barbarism, is participation insofar as participation cannot be objectified."9 This is why he can describe the concrete or existential philosophy that made him so famous as bearing precisely on the thinking thought thus understood, namely, as "based on a datum which is not transparent to reflection, and which, when reflected, implies an awareness not of contradiction but of a fundamental mystery," and a mystery at that in which our Freedom is rooted. For our filling in the blank slate is but a matter of decision based on a free use of our attention and altogether alien to logical necessity and "mediation." "My undeniable ability to pursue or not a sequence of thoughts," he writes, "is, in the final analysis, only a mode of attention, and can be immediately exercised; hence we can confirm the fact that our freedom is implied in the awareness of our participation in the universe."10 And it is precisely in thisregion that "metaphysics joins not so much the ethical but the spiritual life, strictly speaking."11

There is no limit, therefore, to the "I think" of "pensée pensante," which "is valid only if it signifies, in an admittedly loose and inadequate way, an original datum which is not `I think' nor even `I am alive', but rather `I experience,' and this expression must be accepted in its maximal range of indefiniteness."12 To the extent that the consciousness of being able to know all perceptible things entails the ability to perceive them sensibly, he was entitled to refer to our process of knowledge as an all-encompassing process that does not start at the level of thought, but goes down to the level of sensation thereby including the latter in

our spontaneous "self-consciousness." And, if it is
true that knowing amounts to Being affirming itself in
me in all possible ways, it follows that the I
experience is obviously the same as Being experiences
itself in me, making and becoming all things and thereby
laying the foundation for all other spiritual acts. On
the other hand, since love necessarily follows
knowledge, we should feel entitled to limit our research
to the Aristotelian flavor with which Marcel singles out
the acts of knowledge, which are all based on a
fundamental sharing of the soul's actuality. For not
even sensation is to be understood in a merely passive
way according to Marcel, to whom "to receive is not to
fill up a void with an alien presence but to make the
other person participate in a certain plenitude."13 By
insisting that "feeling is not and cannot be passivity,"
Marcel sides most definitely with Aristotle, and he even
acknowledges his bias when he writes: "this view is
opposed to what the philosophical doctrines of the past
have generally maintained, at least when they took issue
with Aristotle who had I think some penetrating views on
the subject."14

2 - Relation Between the Thinking Thought and
    the Conceptualized Thought.

It goes without saying that such an actively
welcoming attitude presupposes that, if the subject must
be able to let the objects of experience become one
reality with it through their sharing its own actuality,
it must itself be an actuality, albeit not a "thing."
There is even a passage in the Metaphysical Journal in
which the thinking thoughtis described as what
Aristotle calls the possible intellect and the latter's

actualization is made dependent both on the active
influence of the data in their capacity as "insufficient
conditions" and on the light of the mind, as will be
shown later. Writes Marcel:

> The thought is not a thing which can
> be juxtaposed to other things.
> Outside these external data it
> cannot be defined for itself, or for
> a thought which tries to understand
> it. Strictly speaking there is no
> dualism of the synthetic act which
> realizes these external data, by
> mediating them, and the external
> data themselves. This is perhaps
> best expressed by saying that the
> external data present a character of
> ideality [within the thinking
> thought]; that is, they define
> themselves from the starting point
> of thought itself (of the whole) as
> conditions both necessary and
> insufficient, that are conditioned
> in their turn by that very thing
> that is conditioned by them.[15]

No doubt his Aristotelian background comes very
handy to Marcel when the latter is engaged in rejecting
the mental passivity that realism attributes to the
subject as well as the almighty activity of the object
in the process of knowledge that according to the
empiricists really takes place. Indeed, if Marcel can
literally reduce the realm of Nature to the realm of the
subject--i.e. not merely conceive of knowledge as a

mirroring of the former in the latter-- it is because,
like the Aristotelian "possible intellect," Marcel's
thinking thought is potentially all things and actually
none. Of course, by thus doing away with the duality
subject-object, he implicitly shows that the problem of
skepticism is nothing but a pseudo-problem. With a
touch of indulging interpretation of Hegel's Logic of
Essence, he even writes:

> This links up, moreover, with Hegel:
> Das Rein innerliche ist das Rein
> ausserliche... Thought cannot really
> have an internal content unless it
> gives it to it as external--it is by
> this mediation of the given that it
> mediates itself; the immediacy of
> thought is correlative to that of
> the object. There is nothing which
> is already mediated, which is given
> as mediated. That would be the
> worst contradiction. And this
> simple reflection is enough to
> destroy completely the idea of a
> thought that is something already.16

However, we should not lose sight of the fact that
the interiorization of the object parallels the process
of the "construction" of the mind; for, as he puts it,
"...the mind, which is constructed, as I have said, by
overcoming exteriority, far from being capable of main-
taining objectively determinable relations with
exteriority, in some way absorbs exteriority into
itself."17 It is clear that such a construction presupposes a condition of possibility which is no other than

the original "constitution" of the spirit. Now, the latter, in Marcel's view, amounts to the constitution of Blondel's pensée pensante, which is such precisely because it consists in an ongoing givenness of Being in its capacity as the Kantian transcendental object=X. As Marcel puts it, "for myself, as for Mr. Maurice Blondel, the pensée pensante can be developed only if it is constantly replenished in such a way that its uninterrupted communication with Being is guaranteed."18 The word "constitution," that figures in the French text, is most significant. It means that the subject is not yet ready to grow and be "constructed" as long as it has not been replenished by Being's givenness. Accordingly, any conceptual system that works independently of the mind fully constituted in this ontological sense is in jeopardy. This is why, days before his death, Marcel strongly warned us that "it is certainly tempting but infinitely dangerous to cut the umbilical cord that binds pensée pensante and pensée pensée. But that is just the temptation a person yields to (unwittingly at that) when he thinks he can reduce a philosophy to the formulas in which to a certain extent it is embodied."19 But, when we speak of the "constitution" of the pensée pensante, we are not talking of any kind of apprehension, not even of the Kantian transcendental apperception, or the medieval concept of "ens." We are talking of a direct participation of the subject in Being which makes possible all our knowing "attitudes" to the extent that they are regulated by a sense of ontological necessity which stems from Being's being directly intuited in itself by the subject. It is at that point that, as Marcel puts it, "the mind only becomes for itself (that is only becomes mind) inasmuch as reality seems to it to be directed by a necessity within it...The mind, I said, only becomes mind on condition it recognises a world of necessity. It does not appear to itself as creating this world, and in reality it does not create it; it discovers it, and in the measure in which it discovers it, it thinks it necessarily as being independent of the act by which it thinks it. The mind in one sense is precisely this discovery..."[20]

To the extent that such a recognition is not an apprehension, it can only be a kind of shower of light coming from Being through the direct intuition of the same, by means of which our acts of knowledge are directed and oriented. That epistemological steering activity, though, is not itself an intuition proper. "Rather than to speak of intuition in this context," writes Marcel, "we should say that we are dealing with an assurance which underlies the entire development of thought, even of discursive thought."[21] In other words, he adds, if "intuition can be mentioned in this context at all, it is not an intuition which is, or can be, given as such. The more an intuition is central and basic in the being whom it illuminates, the less it is capable of turning back and apprehending itself...Hence, any effort to remember such an intuition, to represent it to oneself, is inevitably fruitless. From this point of view, to be told of an intuitive knowledge of being is like being invited to play on a soundless piano."[22]

Undoubtedly, this is a difficult thought; and it is so difficult precisely because it is so much out of the ordinary. Now, it is so odd because it reaches the deepest level of human nature. In this sense, viewing it from Aristotle's De Anima's point of view in which the same issue is at stake, cannot help but shed light on its oddity. Let us go back, therefore, to the bibliographic reference we made at the beginning of section one in this chapter.

This blinded and ongoing intuition, which is but the reverse side of the constitution of the penṡée pensante, of which we will treat in a minute--the latter's active manifestation, we might say--, can only be rooted in the subject itself insofar as, to use Aristotle's frame of thought, having appropriated the light of Being by intentionally becoming the Concrete Universal through the latter's direct grasp and thereby stored it also in itself, it has already gained an exuberance of confidence concerning its own ability to know everything; or, to say it with Marcel in the just quoted sentence, insofar as it is already experiencing an "assurance which underlies the entire development of thought." It would help to realize that this confident subject is precisely what Aristotle had already discovered under the name of the possible intellect and had contrasted with the agent intellect. For the latter was indeed supposed to be the same subject, although in a different capacity, namely, insofar as it could find in that consciousness that it has of itself as a possible intellect and which ensued from such a constitutive intentional transformation of the subject into Being as such, the very light of Being that later on it would have to use as a horizon for all the acts of knowledge in which the actual intelligibility of the object is required. But it is well known that, according to Aristotle, such an illumination cannot be yet what finally clenches the process of intelligibilization of the object. For by letting the percepts, as

they appear, share in such an ontological frame, the
agent intellect prompts their automatic assimilation on
the part of the possible intellect, through which they
finally become actually intelligible to the latter, and
thereby force, so to speak, the possible intellect
actually to understand them. In this sense, the final
degree of actual intelligibility of the object can be
said to depend also and ultimately on the possible
intellect. The active mind--or the subject in its
capacity as "Being intuiting itself" and thereby storing
in itself the ontological light in which alone things
can be understood-- does begin the process of intelligibilization of the object, but the latter actually
comes to an end only when the possible mind actively
bestows upon the object its own actual intelligibility,
that is, its own consciousness of being Being itself on
the intentional level, thereby letting it share in its
own subjective transparence as being also itself a real
being in actuality. This ongoing self-consciousness of
Being in us is the blindfolded knowledge of the same
that is implied in all particular acts of knowledge, as
Marcel has it in his entry of the 26th of June, 1929, of
his Journal Metaphysique.23

All of this amounts to saying that according to
Marcel it is the "pensée pensante" that makes the world
actually intelligible, just as according to Aristotle it
was the agent intellect, in combination with the
possible one, that did it. But by the same token "The
idea of a rational ready-made world that only has to be
rediscovered"--as the realists seem to suggest--"is
really no more than an aspect arbitrarily disassociated
from the complex movement by which the mind is realised
in recognising the world." Marcel, of course, could not

be interested in it. To him, "The idea of a world
completed by the mind, through which it becomes
conscious of itself, is of greater interest. It is a
better safegaurd of the indissoluble unity outside of
which everything ceases to be intelligible."[24]
Ironically, this fully coincides again with Aristotle's
reason for an agent intellect, namely, that things outside the subject are not yet actually intelligible and
must therefore "be made so" by an active factor that
necessarily resides in the soul. Marcel extends that
power of the agent intellect to the actual intelligibility of the very principle of identity. He dismisses the
contention that such a principle belongs to the soul as
an innate possession, for, as he puts it, "the intelligibility that makes that principle what it is, that makes
it valid, does not belong to it objectively, but is
bound to the act by which the mind recognises itself in
it."[25] In fact, itself and every instance of intelligibility—including "that which is" as the supreme norm of
thought— comes down to the other side of the ontological participation that constitutes the pensée pensante.
There cannot be a first and in some way immediate state
of intelligibility if thought does not recognize itself
in it before it is able (in the order of reflection, not
in the order of time) to affirm anything. Hence, intelligibility itself "cannot be defined other than by an
appeal to the very life of thought,"[26] which, as we are
going to see, is participation in Being insofar as
participation cannot be objectified.[27]

3 - The "Pensée Pensante" and the Intuition of
   Being as the Spring of Human Existence.

Upon publishing Du refus à l'invocation in 1940,

Marcel honestly acknowledged that the interpretation of
the "pensée pensante" that he was then introducing to
his readers was purely old wine in new bottles. As we
can see from the following confession, it was only the
name that was new, having been recently borrowed from
Maurice Blondel; and we can even detect in that bit of
history a certain nostalgia for the original designa-
tion, which renders more effectively the aspect of
ontological symbiosis that his conception of the pure
subjectivity entails: "The term `participation,' which I
constantly used between the years1910 and 1914 with a
meaning altogether different from the meaning conferred
on it by Plato, reappears in the philosophy of Mr.
Lavelle, and in some respects is similar to my own use
of the term."[28] Evidently, he is referring to the
famous Fragment XII, which due to a fortunate change of
mind on the part of the Marcel of Creative Fidelity was
luckily published in 1961 and translated by Father
Lionel A. Blain in his Gabriel Marcel, Philosophical
Fragments 1909-1914.[29]

Contrary to Marcel's 1940 rating of his own
manuscript, we find it most enlightening and will use it
as the main source of information at this stage of our
research, all the more so that it sheds light on the
final unadulterated position of Marcel while telling us
a lot about the efforts the latter made to reach the
core of his notion of "Thinking Thought." Ironically,
even the French philosopher himself entices us to study
such a document by describing it in the following
manner: "The difficult task I gave myself then was to
determine the possibility of thinking that participation
without denaturing it, i.e. without converting it into
an objective relation. Doubtless"--he adds with a touch

of modesty or (shall we say?) with a bout of his chronic philosophical disease which was an incurable "perfectionism"--"there is little worth saving in these exploratory writings which have never been published and probably never will. But it should be said that my main views have not changed even if the terminology has."[30]

The very approach to the problem at hand just outlined, as well as the nature of the issue itself, forbade him to use the "positive dialectic" (later on to be called "primary reflection"") that he had been using during his first ontological gropings, and forced him to introduce--perhaps for the first time-- his famous secondary reflection, which at that time was simply called "negative dialectic" and which consists in looking for the conditions of possibility of a fact. In this case, of course, the fundamental fact that was calling for an exhaustive account was our immediate contact with Being without which there would be no genuine act of knowledge whatsoever, but for which in turn at first glance only two alternatives offered themselves as possible accounts: either such a contact was purely logical and dialectical, or it was intuitive and based on an immediate givenness of Being--albeit not an empirical one--, and therefore if its actual reality were still in need of a deduction, it would have to be "deduced," not conceptually through primary reflection, but metaphysically through secondary reflection and on the grounds that besides its admission no other reason would be sufficient to account for the fact at stake. For, as was clearly surmised in Marcel's famous article of 1912, "Les conditions dialectiques de la Philosophie de l'Intuition," from the outset he had strongly hinted that not only would he be able to establish the reality

of such an intuition, but also that perhaps the latter
was precisely what Henri Bergson had had in mind all
along.

In the same article he had even been able to out-
line the method that his secondary reflection would have
to follow. Indeed, since "...to negate Being amounts to
banning it on the grounds that it is alien to thought"
--which it is indeed, if we take "thought" to mean
"conceptual knowledge" --"and thereupon to posit it as
being one with the act which posits it," the right thing
to do first would be to push such a doctrine to its
breaking point by showing that the bottom line of that
thought is an absurdity pure and simple. "Consequently," he wrote, on the one hand, "we must bring to focus
the very act which posits the identity between Being and
its idea. If by thinking itself such an act crumbles
and destroys itself, then a philosophy of intuition is
still viable under certain conditions that we have still
to look for."31 On the other, though, we must embark on
a thorough examination of the subject of a would-be
direct intuition of Being--which would be the only
alternative left--to see whether it is not subject to
any sort of intrinsic contradiction in terms. Obviously, the first step consists in discarding the
"unmentioned" Hegellian way of understanding Absolute
Knowledge, and the second comes down to replacing the
identity "Being-Thought" with an a priori self-affirma-
tion of Being itself in us on the grounds--still to be
shown--that it is a way of understanding absolute knowledge without incurring any absurdity, and that it is
the only one. It goes without saying that, if our
experience is to be unified in one consciousness and
given meaning and validity, absolute knowledge must be

posited as a fact; and that is precisely what Kant calls the transcendental unity of apperception, in which alone things can become actually intelligible. Part of the success, therefore, will depend on the determination of the limits and the scope of the unity of truth, without which no act of thought is possible.

Thus understood, absolute knowledge must go beyond the temporal order without however thereby sharing the same character of "a-temporality" that is enjoyed by an absolute consciousness. This means that, lest we are willing to fall into endless contradictions that we are not about to register here, absolute knowledge cannot be understood as a process to be completed in time. This, of course, leaves us no other choice than to make it "a-temporal" in the sense of an a priori awareness which is logically presupposed to all a posteriori acts of knowledge as their condition of possibility and is therefore not empirically acquired itself--in one word, as the a priori Kantian concept of the ens realissimum which is demanded by the principle of the complete determination of things.32 Furthermore, as an a priori awareness, it is already in our power from the beginning. This fully eliminates any kind of "a-temporal" omniscience, which by force would have to be pinned on an outside mind, because according to the interpretation the act of finite consciousness would presuppose both the positing of that separate absolute consciousness and the reproduction within itself of the content of knowledge of that supreme absolute mind; and this, in turn, would call for a conscious link between finite consciousness and absolute consciousness, an act of awareness that would necessarily have to fall outside the supposedly all-encompassing absolute knowledge. . .

Besides, being a priori, absolute knowledge thus understood must necessarily come out of the subject himself; but then it is its "immanence" that becomes the problem. And a problem indeed it is, and a serious one at that. For the immanence of absolute knowledge in the subject is inseparable from the immanence of Being in thought; or, to put it otherwise, because such an immanent thought would never be able to relate to reality if even prior to any conceptual act it could not grasp the intelligibility of Being one way or the other. But then the question arises: how is Being immanent to thought? Since we have already left behind us the immanence of Being by identity which is advocated by the idealists, the following reasoning becomes unavoidable: if thought necessarily implies Being without thereby being identical with Being, it must by force be understood as taking place "IN" Being; but this makes a real participation of thought in Being a "must."[33] Yet, is this ontological participation really free of any shadow of intrinsic absurdity?

At this point, Marcel was literally torn by conflicting puzzles. For one thing, he could not see how pure subjectivity could be absolutely unknowable—and thus lack all objectivity of its own -- as its participatory status would call for, and yet simultaneously serve as the ground of objectivity for our whole experience, a function which presupposes its being endowed with its own objectivity. At first, only one "problematic" way out seemed to loom on the horizon—a solution that would have to be literally dug from the realization that it is only when pure subjectivity is subjected to a process of objectivization that it appears as a form about which nothing can be said; and an apparently satisfactory solution, at that, on the grounds that such a process of objectivization is itself completely illegitimate since the form that it finally yields when it forces the subject to face up to itself as an object is only an empty form. Yet, that was not quite the desired solution. After all, it is still possible to ask: could it be that such a contradiction lies at the level of the un-objectified pure subject which is being assumed as a fact? In accordance with his most demanding dialectic, Marcel stopped still once more to verify if indeed what he had been calling pure thought was not after all itself a subtle kind of knowledge which works from a privileged position in the sense that it does indeed reach Being itself and therefore can know it first hand. In Marcel's view there was sufficient reason for raising such a puzzle on the grounds that the objectivization of the self is built in "self-consciousness"-- as can be shown by the fact that, in the process of objectifying anything whatsoever, the mind posits the subject as one more object opposite the original object of consideration-- and that consequently such an objectivization would seem to be inseparable from the self's constitution. This is indeed a truth of our own nature, and it must be reconciled with the other truth already encountered, namely, that-- as Kant understood it so well when he made knowledge rest altogether on the presence and givenness of the transcendental object=X34 -- the only living source that can be reasonably assigned to the concrete object of knowledge is the very "thinking thought" understood as the most concrete ontological participation.

Marcel, of course, tried to reconcile these two
truths by stating that the objectifying procedure is
only a provisional step taken by the mind while it is
endeavoring to construct itself in experience, and that
such a step in turn derives a true validity from the
metaphysical value of a more basic notion of which
thematization itself is only a reflection. In other
words, although pure thought is exterior to knowledge,
knowledge too does ultimately participate in Being. Yet
at this point he stumbled upon a new problem. For after
all, he asked himself, if it is true that knowledge
participates in Being through thought, why not say that
it does so as a pure shadow of thought--in which case
knowledge would be but a different and more explicit
appearance of thought and the latter would correlatively
be knowledge not yet in its full appearance, but knowledge nevertheless and by the same token knowable
through reflection? Marcel replied to his own objection
that knowledge participates in Being through thought in
the sense that it is a mere result of thought's full
actualization (which in turn takes place under the
impact of the object)-- in the same way, we might say,
as it certainly does through the Aristotelian possible
intellect's actualization--, but not as thought's mere
waning shadow. It follows therefore that, whereas in
the shadow-type of hypothesis--which he rejected--, the
transition from pure thought to knowledge would take
place through a mere process of explicitation and thus
through a logical operation of thought, in his own
account the transition that makes knowledge both
possible and necessary is not itself an act of knowledge
but a different "way of being" of pure thought. In
other words, it is not as knowledge that thought participates in Being, but only as pure unknowable subject.[35]

The original problem therefore still stands as outlined before: Is thought, as pure participation in Being, intrinsically absurd?

The basic datum for its solution was now evident. It is a fact that the objectivization of pure thought is always accompanied by a clear contradiction. Does this mean that it is objectivization that "creates" such a contradiction, or is it rather that objectivization confines itself to letting a contradiction, which was always and already nestled in the very kernel of pure thought, come to full light? In the first place, according to Marcel we should not waste our time trying to solve this problem through primary reflection since, on the one hand, by definition pure thought is neither an act of intellect nor an act of abstraction based on a previous intellect, whereas, on the other, it is only through intellect and abstraction that primary reflection can ever maintain its hold on anything. In the second place, unlike the notion of square circle, the notion of pure ontological participation on the part of the subject does not show any absurdity in itself and thereby--unlike the notion of square circle again--it flashes the green light to the process of secondary reflection, which seizes the opportunity at once by concluding that either pure thought is posited as the ultimate epistemological foundation, or no objectivity for human knowledge as a whole will ever be found. As a result, we are led to conclude that there is a direct participation in Being and that it is not one more act of knowledge but rather a reality, which gives rise to a real disposition that makes the whole process of knowledge possible--to the kind of blinded intuition that, as already mentioned, Marcel describes as "an assurance which underlies the entire development of thought, even of discursive thought."36

By following the thread of the same secondary reflection that just led us to this conclusion, we might further deepen our understanding of the nature of thinking-thought without ever having to reach the conceptual level. But by the same token we will be forced to join an old metaphysical traditional approach.

Let us start with the realization that the "pensee pensante," or human person, thus understood can only consist of an appearance of Being "to itself." Were it not so understood, the difference between a rock, which in a way is also a direct participation in Being, and a self conceived of, as Marcel suggested, as "a stage in which Being affirms itself," would be barely discernible. Fortunately, Marcel's bias for the latter view is undebatable, and this ranks him with the Oriental philosophers one hundred per cent. For instance, Keiji Nishitani, the great Japanese philosopher who had the opportunity to study under Heidegger and thereby contrast the Buddhist thought with Existentialist Ontology, has been able to explicate the self's directness of involvement in Being in such a way that both Marcel's "pensee pensante" can benefit from it and the human essential tendency to live in a communitarian harmony, where petty selfishness has no room, will find its perfect account.

Indeed, Nishitani clearly traces the notion of person to the manifestation of Being to itself; and he does it in such a way that, although through that unique kind of appearance "no particular thing" appears, still

it can be said to render Being known to itself. He
writes: "Person is an appearance with nothing behind it
making an appearance...That is to say...complete
nothingness, not one single thing, occupies the position
behind the person."37 But, according to him, this is
enough to warrant his use of the word persona in the
Greek sense of "mask." "In this sense"--he points out--
"we can understand person as persona... but only as the
persona of absolute nothingness."38

The implication of this approach is highly
rewarding. For, as this ontological foundation of the
concept of person points, not only to an identity of
origin for all persons (including the divine one), but
also to a common infinitely lovable object, which is
Being, it becomes crystal clear that the actualization
of the potential identity of the selves through love--
which is implied in that original situation-- is also a
real possibility. The end result must be that all
persons are able to love each other because all of them
arise out of the same ground; and in this sense a
correction to the mystical language becomes necessary.
Nishitani affords it at once. Speaking of the mystical
experience he writes: "One cannot really speak here any
longer of `union.' Indeed, Eckhart himself stresses
that it is not a matter of being united with God (Deo
unitum esse) but of being one with God (unum esse cum
Deo). It is, if you will, the self-identity of the soul
that is self-identical with the self-identity of God.
"It brings the soul to a desert of absolute death," he
adds, referring to the realm where there are no "beings"
but where all "beings" are rooted, "and at the same time
discloses a fountainhead `springing up within itself' of
absolute life."39

This entitles us to stretch Marcel's conception of the "pensée pensante," as a direct participation in Being, to God himself insofar as he too is a person. Being, therefore, becomes the unifying ground of all "pensees pensantes." Nishitani, for one, could not help being impressed; and, unwittingly, perhaps, he underscored the wonderful bottom-line of Marcel's conception when he said, referring to Being: "It is at once the source of the eternal life of God and of the eternal life of the soul. In this fountainhead, God and soul are as a single living `pure One.' Elsewhere Eckart expresses it in these terms: `The ground of God is the ground of my soul; the ground of my soul is the ground of God'."[40] In other words, participating in Being amounts to stemming from Being as a finite subject just as the infinite subsistent "pensée pensante," God, did essentially from eternity. It is this being rooted in Being that makes possible our whole experience.

No wonder, therefore, that although it is not an act of knowledge, the ontological participation makes the ontological affirmation possible in all its forms because it asserts its own identity with the epistemological subject of daily life. Indeed, such an assertion amounts to laying the foundation for "the act by which the mind is constituted when it makes actual the freedom immanent in the I think,"[41] i.e. when it assimilates the empirical data under what Kant would call transcendental apperception. All of these characteristics come all wrapped up in the following final paragraph:

Through an act of transcendence
which is above all reflection and is
immediate in the sense that it
transcends all mediation thought
affirms its identity with the
subject; this act is an intellectual
intuition that we shall define as
follows: intellectual intuition is
the act by which thought (as pure
subject) affirms its identity with
the subject of the relation of
knowledge posited as an object.
Thought thus raises the subject of
knowledge up to its own level and
affirms that its own complete
freedom resides in that subject.
Clearly, the intellectual intuition
is the preliminary condition of
faith and inaugurates a new type of
intelligibility.[42]

One is also tempted to add that it is this wonderful
intuition, which ensues from the full constitution of
the pure thought, that makes possible also the medita-
tive attitude presupposed by Parmenides' _true_ _belief_, at
least to the extent that the latter, by disregarding the
appearances for a moment, concentrates its attention on
the ontological aspect of the object.

footnotes

[1]See: Marcel, Creative Fidelity, 1974, pp. 13-38. [CrF].

[2]See: Peccorini, F.L., "An Inquiring Response to Professor Tracy's and Professor Baille's Essays On Aristotle," in Ultimate Reality and Meaning, 5(1982), n. 3, pp. 265-271.

[3]Marcel, "Les conditions dialectiques de la philosophie de l'intuition," in Revue de Métaphysique et de Morale, 9 (1912) [CDPI], p. 651.

[4]Marcel, Creative Fidelity, [CrF], 1974, p. 30.

[5]Ibid.

[6]CrF, p. 21.

[7]Marcel, Being and Having [BH], 1965, p. 171.

[8]Marcel, The Philosophy of Existentialism, [PhEx], 1956, p. 18.

[9]CrF, p. 23.

[10]Ibid.

[11]Ibid.

[12]O.c., p. 16.

[13]O.c., p. 28.

[14]Ibid. See also: Gabriel Marcel interrogé par Pierre Boutang, 1977, pp. 75-76.

[15]Marcel, Metaphysical Journal [MJ], 1952, p. 115.

[16]O.c., p. 113.

[17]O.c., p. 124; see also p. 1.

[18]CrF, p. 13.

[19]Marcel, Tragic Wisdom and Beyond [TrW], 1973, p. 189. See MJ, p. 2.

[20]MJ, p. 103.

[21]PhEx, p. 25.

[22]Ibid.

[23]BH, p. 28.

[24]MJ, p. 108.

[25]O.c., pp. 106-107.

[26]O.c., p. 107.

[27]CrF, p. 23.

[28]O.c., p. 21.

[29]See Philosophical Fragments 1909-1914 [PhFr], 1965, pp. 66-67 and 70-77.

[30]Ibid.

[31]CDPI [1912], p. 547, footnote.

[32]See Peccorini, F.L., On to the World of Freedom. A Kantian Meditation on Finite Selfhood (Washington, D.C.: The University Press of America, 1982), pp. 229-232.

[33]See MJ, pp. 106-107.

[34]See Peccorini, O.c., chapters III and IV.

[35]See PhFr [1965], Fragment XII, p. 73.

[36]PhEx, p. 25. See also pp. 17-19.

[37]Keiji Nishitani, Religion and Nothingness. Translated with an introduction by Jan Van Bragt and foreworded by Winston I. King (Berkeley: University of California Press, 1982), p. 70.

[38]O.c., p. 71.

[39]O.c., pp. 62-63.

[40]O.c., p. 63.

[41]MJ, p. 61.

[42]PhFr, p. 82.

Chapter III

Faith and Freedom: The Foundation of Knowledge

Marcel's negative dialectic has just led us to the quintessence of our individuality and our freedom, the two of them now appearing as being only two aspects of the same power of subsuming particulars under the a priori concept of being, and that is the power of what Marcel calls "transcendence." This freedom, on the other hand, does not mean only that the Cogito can be transcended on our way towards metaphysical realities and therefore in a non-conceptual way; it means also that conceptual transcendence is neither unique -- in the sense of the same for everybody-- nor even necessary, since, as Lonergan has shown so well in the footsteps of Aristotle and St. Thomas, it is possible to dwell for a whole lifetime on the level of the sort of Cogito that works only on the perceptual level.

1 - Perception and the Pure Subject: the Birth of Freedom.

Jeanne Delhomme concurs on this. She writes: "No one is ever being forced to go beyond the Cogito; there is nothing compelling in its constitution, nothing that would prevent us from engulfing ourselves in the immediate. And if formal thought can catch a glimpse of a beyond ahead of it, it is because it can lean on the pure freedom from which it stemmed in the first place, on an I which was not there all set and ready-made. And yet, its being free does not entail that it is arbitrary and that both the gratuity of the choice and the swings of indecision are essential to it. Because it is both creative and reflexive, it is possible for it to detect in its own activity a drive and an appeal coming from singularity, even while the latter is being smothered by the universality. This drive and this appeal take the form of a will and a power to think otherwise and they have their roots in a certain protest of our individuality, which is neither universalizable nor verifiable."[1]

It is precisely our being able to think otherwise throughout the endless endeavor of accounting for the whole reality that makes the Cogito reformable and corrigible within its realm--which is the realm of empirical universal concepts--and the self one hundred percent free to transcend it in all directions. As Quine has seen it so well--and Immanuel Kant would be ready to confirm it with the flexibility of his Critique of Judgment "vis-à-vis" the "appearances" of things[2]-- "We can improve our conceptual scheme, our philosophy, bit by bit while continuing to depend on it for support; but we cannot detach ourselves from it and compare it objectively with an unconceptualized reality. Hence it is meaningless, I suggest, to inquire into the absolute correctness of a conceptual scheme as a mirror of reality."[3] Marcel, too, was impressed by the same philosophical freedom. "I am of the firm belief," he wrote in his Metaphysical Journal, "and my conviction is not of recent date, that Philosophical truths are relative to the requirements (exigences) of the thoughts that constitute them. The hierarchy of truths is defined in function of the hierarchy of requirements."[4] He accounted for such a variety on the basis of the variegated aspects that the same datum is able to show, depending on its relations to the different aspects of reality that are to be accounted for and which are already and always open to the mind in what we might call the apperception of its possible experience. This is why he wrote that "From the standpoint of the higher planes the immediate must no longer be defined as a datum but as infinitely mediable. This does not mean that it ceases to be a datum, but that the category of datum is not here the essential thing. The relation of the Gegebensein on which in the beginning all, it was claimed, could be built, is shown to be entirely devoid of intrinsic significance, in the sense that it implies an empirical subject who himself enfolds an infinite."[5]

We thereby wind up once again at the door of pure thought insofar as the latter does always and already participate in the infinity of Being--insofar as it is one with the "empirical subject who himself enfolds an infinite," as Marcel just told us. And, as we further penetrate into the thick wilderness of Marcel's early entries in his Journal Métaphysique, as we are doing now, we come to realize that pure thought begins to loom all the more as the true ultimate reality and meaning which accounts for all aspects of human existence.

Indeed, it is in pure subjectivity that freedom keeps smoldering under the warm breath of Being--which gave it birth in the first place--and manifesting itself through the ongoing and magic-blinded intellectual intuition which also constitutes "the preliminary condition of faith"-- as Marcel told us in Fragment XII-- and

"by which thought (as pure subject) affirms its identity
with the subject of the relation of knowledge posited as
an object." In fact, these few lines of Fragment XII
contain the seed of the solution to Marcel's fundamental
problem, which was no other than the problem of philosophy at large, namely, the puzzling question that has
tormented for centuries the idealists and the
empiricists alike.

It is precisely the question that Kant tackled so
decisively and to which he gave a solution very much
like the one that Marcel is going to find insofar as it
resorts to an a priori constitution of the same self
regardless of whether the latter is being considered on
the level of thought or on the empirical level. It
could be formulated in this way: assuming that if we had
only what Kant calls the pure understanding and Marcel
designates as the Cogito we would at most be able to
apprehend things as beings and substances only, but not
as trees and rocks,[6] what then is it that enables us to
subsume natural entities under the concept of "being"?
In other words, to use Marcel's Journal Métaphysique
once again, "On what conditions can the Cogito transcend
itself? And first and foremost, what makes the act of
transcendence possible?[7] We all daily experience such
an undeniable transcendence, but no one will ever be
able to conceptualize it. Marcel himself, in a state of
bewilderment, recognizes that "Between the empirical
content which is the datum given to the I think--and by
reflection on which the I think is constituted--and the
I think itself, no relation is thinkable."[8] Thinking--
in the sense of knowing conceptually--is here the key
word. He knows, of course, that some efforts have been
made in the past to "interpret" such a relation and

thereby "convert" the I think into a form, but to no avail because those efforts necessarily had to remain on the surface: "Pure formalism," he says, "has the extremely serious defect of being unable to account for the act that makes it possible; for the act by which the conversion of the Cogito into form is operated--and indirectly for the cogito itself."[9] He is equally aware that the idealists tried to do away with the relationship itself altogether, but he cannot be satisfied with their solution either because in his view our blinded intuition belies such a claim at once. "What relation"--he asks--"can I establish between myself as thinking, and myself as empirical, that is to say, in so far as I enfold the universe, for between me and the world there are infinitely complex relations in which, in last analysis, all reality is involved?"[10] On the other hand, the empiricists may be farther away from the mark inasmuch as they try to obtain the Cogito--i.e. the concept of being--through induction entirely overlooking that induction itself cannot take place without the use of such a concept. "Can I deny that there is a relation?"--he wonders, making the transition from his diatribe against the idealists to the empiricists' misconception, and then he adds--""Or can I try to derive the thinking ego from the empirical ego? This solution," he goes on, "as we already know, is not acceptable. It takes on a semblance of coherence only by substituting for the act of I think a complex psychism with which this act (inasmuch as it is intelligible and unverifiable) cannot and should not be confused. To be possible, the truth of the relation that we are claiming to establish requires the Cogito itself, and the problem consists in integrating the cogito into an empirical synthesis."[11] The gibe at

Locke's derivation of universal concepts is not too subtlely hidden.

As a result he is cornered to the following solution: "From this we would have to conclude that thought must posit the relation of the I think to the empirical order as unverifiable, that is, it must affirm the absolute impossibility of an objective definition (even, in fact above all, a dualistic one) of such a relation."[12] In other words, pure thought affirms entirely a priori and without any logical deduction that the I think and the I perceive are one and the same subject in which its own complete freedom resides. In Marcel's view, therefore, transcendence constitutes the fundamental "unverifiable," but, by the same token, "If, then, the relation of the Cogito to the empirical ego is unverifiable (that is to say, not susceptible of truth), we posit at least the possibility of faith" and we must say that the transition from absolute indetermination to the act of faith "must be regarded entirely free."[13]

2 - Faith and Freedom.

The fact that we have just encountered the possibility of faith as a corollary of the unverifiability of transcendence seems to show that faith is but a special kind of transcendence parallel to, but not identical with, the way of perception. They are parallel insofar as both constitute a case of transcendence, and yet not identical insofar as both are differently related to their respective objects, for whereas "In one instance, ...the act of perception can and must be thought as contingent in relation to the object perceived"--insofar as the latter can precede the former in existence--, we must say that in the case of faith "I need to affirm that the act of believing is constitutive..."14   But more important still is the fact that if transcendence can suggest the possibility of faith ιt is precisely because transcendence itself, which is the bottom line of perception, is a clear case of faith in which the essential characteristics of the latter can be fully understood.

Keeping in mind that transcendence consists in the fact that the Cogito gets transcended at one point or another and in one way or another, we can see that faith fully qualifies as a case of transcendence. "Faith"-- says Marcel--"is the act by which the mind fills the void between the thinking ego and the empirical ego."15 Others, like Sciacca, would concur by saying that it is through personal acts of transcendence such as knowledge, love, and faith, that the spirit grows and becomes what it will be, starting with the blank slate point of the subject (the Aristotelian possible intellect, in fact), and that such a growth constitutes the life of the spirit, which is a mystery, the mystery of the freedom of life. Marcel too points to such a prominent aspect of transcendence. The expression that he purposefully uses, "the mind fills the gap," is indeed already eloquent enough to suggest that the link between the thinking subject and the empirical one (in the sense of the principle of knowledge) is not a logical one. And yet, its free character is so important that it is taken over once again with renewed emphasis by our philosopher in a way that leaves no room for doubt. "The unity [of the thinking ego and the empirical ego that the mind affims so as to be mind]"-- he says--"is in function of the will that wills it."16

We may conclude, therefore, that freedom is inseparable from the essence of transcendence and part of the mystery of the latter. Freedom, but not arbitrariness. For "the transcendental unity is capable of appearing as non-arbitrary, as _valid_, but only as valid for the mind, that is for thought which has transcended itself, for the being that wills to be mind." It is at this point that the essence of perception opens the door to the persistent skepticism about the existence of the world that has literally plagued modern western philosophy ever since the latter repudiated its nuptial bond with Being. And it could not have been otherwise, since the bottom line of perception is an act of faith in Being; and this makes the problem of the actual existence of the external world a pseudo-problem, to use Marcel's own words.

The rooting of perception in Being's presence upon which we just stumbled sheds plenty of light on the next remark of the _Metaphysical_ _Journal_: "In this way we can at least conceive the relation of human freedom to divine freedom which is the central mystery of the Christian religion."[17] Indeed, if the divine Self is merely Being as Freedom in a state of infinite self-consciousness and pure thought is Being as Freedom in a state of finite self-consciousness and, furthermore, if not doubting our perceptions comes down to freely accepting Being's testimony in us, and that, to the extent that Being as it is in us is due to the remote presence of Being as God, then it is possible for us to extend our consent also to the Being of God if the implication of the latter is our Being ever becomes clear to us. Religion, therefore, depends on a free act, but the latter in made possible by an ontological attitude, which is the antithesis of the hypercritical mind's attitude and of which we shall talk later. Furthermore, from this point of view, the faith in God--which is made possible by our faith in Being--is inseparable from the faith in our own creatural status. This is why Marcel goes on to assert: "In this way...we can finally grasp how the individuality that faith requires as its pivot is created."[18] In other words, we can understand how this finite and individual participation in Being that I am cannot be independent of the will of the One who is Being. Moreover, I can see how my own growth as a mind that fully recognizes its own ontological foundations--in one word, my own religious growth--cannot divorce itself from God's continuing help, and Marcel says it most clearly: "The mind, as we have said, is only created as mind by faith in God. But this faith in God involves the affirmation that is itself conditioned by God, that is to say, the affirmation of the divine fatherhood. Which means that the mind posits God as the positer."[19] This essentially says that the mind can posit God, not only because it has been given to participate in Being but also because God posited me from eternity, which is indeed the case since such a constitutive participation would never have occurred if the one who is Being had not first freely affirmed in his mind the individual person that I am thereby singling me out for the honor of actually participating in Being. And once we have reached this point, it is easy to agree with the following Marcellian statement that refers to Le Quattuor en fa dièze: "...to adopt the words I put into the mouth of Clarisse, God is that in which thoughts communicate, the real foundation of the communication between individualities."[20] Which is the same as to say that the real human community which is demanded by the moral law cannot be alive and healthy if it is not conscious of its divine foundation. In the light of the preeminent role that he had to assign to God or Being as the Absolute "I" in the Metaphysical Journal, the hesitations that he confessed to Pierre Boutang--although they never reached to the point of denial--make little sense, to say the least.[21]

At this point we can pause to recapitulate what we have gotten through our research. One thing cannot be denied, and that is that it is pure thought that alone can account for everyday acts of thought, whether the latter are universal or concrete. As he puts it: "Such thought is exercised in the search for truth and...is the source of our universal judgments."[22] On the other hand, while making all of them possible, it shares with them the seal of freedom that belongs essentially to it. "Thought"--says Marcel--"thus raises the subject of knowledge up to its own level and affirms that its own complete freedom resides in that subject."[23] There is no incompatibility, therefore, between the freedom of Being and the assurance of knowledge since the same pure thought that affirms its freedom in the epistemological subject, as we have just mentioned, gives rise to "an assurance which underlies the entire development of thought, even of discursive thought."[24] Freedom, in other words, can be found both in Faith and in the pure Cogito, that is to say, in all acts of transcendence-- and in none of them does it even entail error--, but the extent to which the latter participates in Freedom varies from plenitude (in faith) to even partial self-suppression. As Marcel puts it: "While science is the concern of the abstract ego, the Cogito, and as a result reposes on the act of a freedom which has not yet

reached the stage of being for itself, religion is based
on the very mind itself, that is to say on the indivi-
dualised thought which has posited an intimate relationship between itself (as abstract) and its integral
experience, by means of the act of faith."[25] This means
that the act of faith is Freedom one hundred per cent:
"The freedom realised in the act of faith is no longer
the virtual freedom of the cogito which is suppressed in
its object; it is actual freedom, freedom for its own
sake."[26] But by the same token it is only through faith
that the excruciating research of the self can find rest
because it is only through faith that pure thought can
exhaust the full revelation contained in the presence of
Being. "Through faith"--says Marcel--"I affirm a transcendental foundation for the union of the world and of
my thought, I refuse to think myself as purely abstract,
as an intelligible form hovering over a world which is
what it may be, and in which necessity is only the
reverse of contingency."[27] Obviously, from the point of
view of the success of the pure thought's concerns,
Marcel is entitled to say that "Thus the order of
science is relative to faith in the measure in which the
I think is subordinated to the I believe--where abstract
thought (the thinking subject) is subordinated to the
mind."[28]

This superiority, though, is quite compatible with
the physical possibility of denial. Indeed, faith is
not prompted by any kind of necessary deduction; it
springs essentially under the overpowering siege that
Being is constantly waging against pure thought within
the core of the self.[29] And this goes for all kinds of
faith if it is true that faith is but the self's
response to the beckoning of Being at three basic levels

where the Cogito has no access, namely, at the level of
the ontological affirmation, at the level of the very
Cogito's transcendence with which we have been dealing
thus far, and at the level of metaphysics, to which
Religion itself belongs. And this is why the pure
Cogito will never be able to account for the act of
faith, it being conversely true that if ever the Cogito,
while analyzing an act of faith, falls into the illusion
of having succeeded in accounting for it, then that
cannot be a true act of faith. We might therefore
simplify the concept of faith by saying that it is the
kind of transcendence of the Cogito that cannot be
credited to the Cogito itself. Marcel can therefore add
that "inasmuch as the act of faith is still attributed
to the Cogito (the universal thinking subject), it is
inevitably defined as a kind of plausible hypothesis, it
is not really faith--it is still as it were in function
of a truth, and appears as its potential approxima-
tion."[30] And he specifies also that if this failure is
honestly recognized by the Cogito, the true essence of
faith comes all of a sudden under the best possible
light to realize it. That light appears at the point
where reflection, desperately having run parallel to the
act of faith that it was bent on accounting for, finally
is forced to realize that it will never be able to meet
it on a common ground. Marcel puts it thus: "in the
process the act of faith seems to be pushed back beyond
all limits (beyond a reflective process that is necessarily endless), and it seems to reflection that it
could only put an end to the regress by self-suppression. Hence the idea of grace, of a power that limits
reflection by suppressing it from without."[31] This is
the moment at which logic is transcended altogether.
Consequently faith remains on its own, and obviously its

value in terms of certainty comes to the focus.

3 - Ontological appetite and Certainty.

In order to find the ultimate foundation of faith,
let us place ourselves at the level of the ontological
affirmation, which is the level of the fundamental kind
of faith. But this forces us to realize that "We are in
the order of freedom, that is to say, in the order of
that which is capable of not being"[32] and that consequently it would be against the rules of the game to
account for thought's transcendence at this level in
terms of a principle of interior conditioned necessity,
thereby letting the objection of arbitrariness besiege
us. Marcel, in a superb ad hominem and cutting retort,
reminds us that as long as the objection refers to
"logical necessity" alone--that is, to a necessity conditioned and depending on laws--, it would be well to
remark that not even logical necessity itself is
"logically necessary" --if it is true that logical
necessity is convertible with the necessity of the first
principles of reason which is altogether "uncondi-
tioned," and therefore "free." "The universality
appertaining to the I think" --he points out--"is not
even--we must take care here--the purely hypothetical
universality that appertains to a law. It is uncondit-
ioned. And unconditionality is the mark of freedom."[33]
In a wonderful "ancora" he even insists on the same
disappointing fact, that is, on the ensnarement of the
logical mind in the webs of metaphysics: "So even if we
limit ourselves to the Cogito"--he adds--"we are for all
that in the metaphysical order, that is to say the order
of freedom."[34] Furthermore, to the extent that there
would be no logical necessity without the freedom of the

faith in the ontological affirmation, we are entitled to set forth the following conclusion: the ontological affirmation, although not logically necessary, is nevertheless most certainly indispensable.

This conclusion is indeed the antithesis of the nihilist's pessimism, which is based on the extrapolation of individual and isolated cases of despair. Marcel, toying with the concepts of "being possible" and "being valid," writes: "And so we will be told: `This absolute pessimism is possible.' There is a sense in which being can be denied. But who can say that this sense is not final? that such pessimism is not valid."[35] He accepts the challenge and goes immediately to work on the nihilist's contention. He even shows full readiness to comply with the demands of his adversary in order to convince him-- a supererogatory effort indeed since the whole Fragment XII sufficiently does the job--, a goal that he plans to pursue by means of the following method: "To be converted (in the purely rational sense)"--he notes--"the pessimist would need a fact (which reflection could to some extent support rather than see through in order to lose itself in non-being, a fact on which to end up)."[36] In his view the needed fact is not only a reality; it was even presupposed by the very attitude of the pessimist himself. For "to say that the universe leaves me dissatisfied, and that in this sense it `is not' is to admit that within me there is an appetite for being."[37] Now, such an appetite could not be better founded since it is inseparable from faith, the foundation of which--as established before-- is the ontological participation that constitutes the pure subject. From here Marcel can go in different directions and find in pure thought, and therefore in

Being, the ultimate foundation of not only human knowledge but also human love, hope, and the feeling of
immortality. It is worth noting that love, hope, and
the feeling of immortality intertwine with one another
and thereby they mutually reinforce and buttress themselves. Ultimately, their whole web of interactions
rests on the infallible nature of the will, if we may
call it that, which lends a certain epistemological
value both to love and to hope.

The will is, we might say, the part of our Being
that is responsible for the effectiveness of its growth and
perfection. This aspect of the nature of the will is
clear in Marcel's famous distinction between desire and
will. Now, from this point of view, the ontological
appetite, which is one of the two necessary manifestations of the inner presence of Being in pure thought--
the other one being the certainty of faith--cannot help
but lend all its value to the will, with which it is
one. Consequently, in its capacity as the purest manifestation of the ontological appetite, the will does not
work at the level of the modality of possibility but
rather in relation to the modality of necessity. Hence
Marcel's description: "to will is to refuse to ask the
question of possibility, or at least it is to refuse to
treat it as primary. In this sense volition implies the
equivalent of a judgment incontestably demonstrated (for
when I say `This or that is necessary' I do not ask
myself whether this or that can be). To will means in
some way to place ourselves beyond the point at which we
can distinguish the possible from the impossible."38
The antithesis he presents between the will,thus
described, and desire necessarily reinforces our understanding of the true nature of the former. For, just as

opinion falls short of knowledge and faith due to its entanglement with lack of certainty, so desire, in Marcel's view, is essentially different from will because it is literally plagued with doubts. As he puts it: "The buts of the man who would like to will and does not will always bear on conditions that are thought as existent and as incompatible with the achievement in question."[39]   But in both these couples--"opinion-knowledge" and "desire-will"--it is the relation of the object to my own Being, in the latter's capacity as a direct participation in Being, that constitutes the determining factor.   Indeed, whereas the object of opinion and desire does not belong to the subject, faith and will bear only on the person's Being. Confining himself to the contrast "faith-will," Marcel clearly formulates that principle in terms of two different ecstasies of time which allow for a true symmetry; for, as he writes in the Metaphysical Journal, "whereas will is brought to bear on what cannot be save through me, faith is brought to bear on that by which I am.'[40] But he does not overlook the fact that from the point of view of Being the ecstasies of time are irrelevant.   "To be sure"--he says--"there is a difference between will and faith: indeed will seems to bear on what is to be, faith on what is.   But the `present'(?) of the object of faith certainly cannot be contrasted with the future of an object of willing as a now can be contrasted with a later."[41]   What ultimately counts is that both essentially disregard what amounts to the same question: "The question that the will sets aside is that of knowing whether a given action can be accomplished; the question that faith refuses to ask is: `Is it really possible?'"[42] In so doing, both of them repudiate the modality of the possible and stay within the modality of necessity, and they do so because of the presence of Being through the presence of my Being to myself; and this, in turn, is the result of the ontological partici- pation that constitutes my own interiority. "I aspire to participate in this being"--writes Marcel in the Ontological Mystery--"in this reality--and perhaps this aspiration is already a degree of participation, how- ever rudimentary."[43] It follows therefore that both in faith and in will my own reality must be brought to bear on them one way or the other, as he illustrates so well in connection with the act of willing. "It seems to me" he says-"that will is in some way to commit oneself: by which I mean to commit or bring into play one's own reality; to throw oneself into what one wills. I would be tempted to go so far as to say that to will is to affirm: `I depend on that (I will only be if that is), hence that depends on me.' But of course this I and this me are not really identical; between them there is a synthetic relation."[44]

In other words, myself and the willed object are so intertwined with one another, that my empirical ego won't ever grow successfully if "that" is not; but, by the same token, the full meaning of "that" won't be grasped if its being called upon to serve as the landing place of my metaphysical ego's transcendence is left out. And although he recognizes that "It is hard to see anything of this kind in faith"-- however he adds some- thing that reminds us of God's immanence in us when he says: "Yet I can only have faith in what I am or, to be more exact, in that by which I am. I mean that faith could not have bearing on a metaphysical order that was radically foreign to me (any more than I would be able really to will something in which my being was not concerned)."45 Finally, the substantial coincidence between faith and will makes them inseparable from one another. "When faith ceases to be love it congeals into objective belief in a power that is conceived more or less physically. And love which is not faith (which does not posit the transcendence of the God that is loved) is only a sort of abstract game. Just as the divine reality corresponds to faith (the former can only be a function of the latter), so divine perfection corresponds to love."46

4 - The Mechanics of Love.

This quotation introduces us to the mechanics of love, which ultimately amounts to an attitude towards Being insofar as Being is good, and therefore to Being's perfection which is to be found only in God.47

It is easy to understand that from the sublime point of view that Marcel has just taken the so-called problem of evil looms awfully petty. This prompts him to write: "The believer does not ask himself--he refuses to ask himself--whether divine perfection is incompossible with the imperfections of the universe as it is presented to him; the man who wills refuses to ask himself if what he wishes to do is compatible with the `drawbacks' of every kind that he observes in and around him.  In both cases I indicate this `overcoming' by the expression `act of transcendence'."48 And to the extent that the pure subjectivity of the other participates in Being and that all love is love of Being, this goes also for the love of one another, where the beloved one's defects, far from alienating the lover, prompt in him renewed and confident efforts towards the former's improvement. Marcel recognizes the fact and accounts for it: "only for love is the individuality of the beloved immune against disintegration and crumbling away, so to speak, into the dust of abstract elements"-- he tells us in the Metaphysical Journal--"But it is only possible to maintain the reality of the beloved"--he goes on to add--"because love posits the beloved as transcending all explanation and all reduction. In this sense it is true to say that love only addresses itself to what is eternal, it immobilizes the beloved above the world of genesis and vicissitude."[49] It is not diffi-cult for Marcel to show that the true lover grows in freedom the more he loves his neighbor "in God," and that one is thereby set free from the need to judge and criticize and finds one's way open towards the love of Being, in which all our confidence must rest. This, of course, prompts the following description of love: "love bears on what is beyond essence, love is the act by means of which a thought [in Marcel's parlance this means a person] by thinking a freedom, is m ade free. In this sense love extends beyond any possible judgment, for judgment can only bear on essence--and love is the very negation of essence (in this sense it implies faith in the perpetual renewal of being itself, the belief that nothing ever can be irremediably lost."[50] And this description, in turn, points in the direction of the infinity of the object of love, which is Being without any essential limitations and confines.

It would seem, therefore, that only the act of willing and loving bears on Being within the modality of necessity, because only in that case can the subject say that what is actually being willed is necessary for its own Being, and that consequently any other use of the

will has to be bent upon the modality of possibility and
is therefore of a lesser status. But this conclusion
necessarily leads us to pose a very puzzling question:
shall we say that, according to the following definition
that we find timidly surmised in the Ontological Mystery
hope is looked down upon within Marcel's philosophy?
"Could not hope therefore"--he writes-- "be defined as
the will when it is made to bear on what does not depend
on itself?"[51] Yet, such an alarm may be premature. In
fact, it overlooks the distinction between something
being necessary for our Being and something being within
the reach of our will. The object of hope may well be
necessary to our Being and still find itself beyond the
reach of our freedom and absolutely dependent on God's
omnipotence. In fact, in hope the former characteristic
does not seem to be missing. Indeed, indirectly as it
may be, even hope can be shown to belong to the category
of necessity, if the following quotation, which enables
us to retrieve the modality of necessity through
reflection, is any indication: "Hope seems to me," he
writes, "as it were, the prolongation of an activity
which is central--that is to say, rooted in being."[52]

5 - Hope and Fidelity.

This suggestion, which consists in a reductive
process, could not be more interesting. Elsewhere he
elaborates on it by introducing the concept of faith. He
starts with the concept of fidelity. An act of fidelity
is an act of will to cling to a promise because so doing
is necessary for my Being. "The fact is"--he says--"that
when I commit myself, I grant in principle that the
commitment will not again be put in question. And it is
clear that this active volition not to question some-

thing again intervenes as an essential element in the determination of what in fact will be the case."[53] There is no doubt that since fidelity implies an "active volition" we are altogether within the modality of necessity. What is being willed on the grounds that it contributes to my ontological perfection does indeed consist in a relation, but the commitment is being undertaken because it counts with a sufficient ground. "At present"--he says--" we may note that all fidelity is based on a certain relation which is felt to be inalterable, and therefore on an assurance which cannot be fleeting."[54]

With this we have already the three elements of a vow. One is the act of will to fulfill our commitment insofar as doing so is necessary for my Being; the other is the motive for such a commitment, which is love. Concerning love as a motive, Marcel describes love in Being and Having as "Charity thought as presence, as absolute disposability."[55] This definition also shows that love is the best possible motive precisely because it is the reason why the commitment based on it is so necessary for my own Being. Indeed, on the one hand, my Being essentially calls for its own perfection, whereas, on the other, my perfection must be dependent on the degree of availability that I show through my behavior, if--as the quotation suggests-- it is the case that being disposable is the best way to imitate God's perfection, which consists precisely in infinite charity in the sense of absolute disposability. Finally, in the third place, a solid ground is mentioned as indispensable if the possible disappointment that is always lurking in the future is to be avoided. In connection with this foundation we read in Creative

Fidelity: "the more my consciousness is centered on God
himself, evoked--or invoked--in his real being...tne
less conceivable this disappointment will be."[56] In his
William James Lectures, pointing to the underlying act
of faith which is built into the act of hope, Marcel
explained: "This assurance is valid, for it is in the
order not of desire, but of hope...The attempt to
silence it would be to shut ourselves within that circle
of fatality...from which we must... release ourselves:
we are m en only on that condition."[57] In other words,
we should not overlook the fact that included in the
object of the act of will--to keep a commitment forever
in an unalterable way--there is a strong act of faith
through which the divine support is supposed to work.
It is indeed a real act of faith because the assurance
of God's help must be taken for granted as a virtual
fact on the grounds that it is essential to our Being,
that is to say, that man cannot be authentically human
as long as he is not supported by the incorruptible
frame of the sacred[58] in his struggle to keep alive his
constant alertness against the spirit of abstractness;[59]
and it is obvious that such a faith cannot fail to
prompt an act of hope, which necessarily converts the
original fidelity into an Absolute Fidelity. Indeed,
the direct object of my faith, namely, God's unfailing
solicitous presence, is directly related to the ensuing
act of hope. Marcel surmises as much when he writes:
"Can I define God as absolute presence [disposability]?
This would embrace my idea of absolute succour."[60]
"Hence"--he concludes--"this ground of fidelity which
necessarily seems precarious to us as soon as we commit
ourselves to another who is unknown, seems on the other
hand unshakable when it is based not, to be sure, on a
distinct apprehension of God as someone other, but on a

certain appeal delivered from the depths of my own insufficiency ad summam altitudinem; I have sometimes called this the absolute resort [succour]."61 Thus, through the analysis of the act of absolute fidelity, Marcel has just brought us to "the juncture of the most stringent commitment and the most desperate expectation." He has shown that so astounding a juncture is indeed possible if we have faith in God's absolute fidelity. "It cannot be a matter of counting on oneself, of one's own resources, to cope with this unbounded commitment;"--he says--"but in the act in which I commit myself, I at the same time extend an infinite credit to Him to whom I did so; Hope means nothing more than this.."62

6 - Recollection and Virtue.

It is time now to stop and look back. The first thing that strikes us is that the conditions of possibility of so many and so important features of human existence--logic, perception, faith, the metaphysical value of the ontological appetite and of the moral law, as well as love, hope, and absolute fidelity--do in fact reduce to one, namely, the makeup of the human subject as pure thought and its direct participation in Being. The implications of the agreement on the part of each one of us with the foregoing scheme are decisive indeed: if it takes place, skepticism, for sure, will be wiped out altogether from our minds; the moral law won't encounter the least reluctance on the part of the will and society will be all the better for that; if it does not, doubt and mistrust will pervade human existence on all levels. Yet the magic agreement itself, required as it is for such a good scenario to ensue, does not stand a chance if a certain disposition that Marcel calls "recollection" is not adopted. It is indeed so socratically oriented a disposition that Marcel could once say with full truth: the ways that lead to metaphysics and the ones that wind up in holiness must in the end come to a meeting point.[63]

The support for his stand comes through the following penetrating analysis: "the ontological order can only be recognised personally by the whole of a being, involved in a drama which is his own, though it overflows him infinitely in all directions--a being to whom the strange power has been imparted of asserting or denying himself. He asserts himself in so far as he asserts Being and opens himself to it; or he denies himself by denying Being and thereby closing himself to it. In this dilemma lies the very essence of his freedom."[64] This, of course, is tantamount to pinning on human existence a meaning fraught with risk and tragic dramatism.

Recollection, therefore, should be described as an attitude of heeding only our genuine natural inclinations and acting always realistically by never trespassing the limits of our truly human resources. To be more specific, the decisive factor in all our decisions should be the fact that human nature comes down to the essential participation upon which we insisted so much in chapter II of this book. Now, since the unavoidable manifestation of the ontological constitution of our subjectivity is the pervasive blinded intuition that made Marcel so famous--which is so unavoidable indeed that it even constitutes the worst harassment for the professed proselytist nihilist--, the best guarantee of human behavior must necessarily coincide with a constant awareness of the fact that, wittingly or not, all our spontaneous reflections in life are prompted by our ontological participation, and therefore they ought to be traced back to it if their validity is to be successfully verified. But it is precisely that return to our ontological foundations that takes, if not virtue, at least a gigantic decision. We are dealing here with a resolute disregard of the enticing sirens of objectivity as well as of our dependence on our life and we are trying to replace our objective attitude with one of centering on ourselves by means of what Marcel calls "recollection." For "It is within recollection"--he writes in On the Ontological Mystery-- "that I take up my position--or, rather, I become capable of taking up my position-- in regard to my life; I withdraw from it in a certain way, but not as the pure subject of cognition; in this withdrawal I carry with me that which I am and which perhaps my life is not." Such a withdrawal is certainly not an easy task for us who happen to live within a world which only values objectivity. Indeed, "Recollection is doubtless what is least spectacular in the soul; it does not consist in looking at something, it is an inward hold, an inward reflection, and it might be asked in passing whether it should not be seen as the ontological basis of memory-- that principle of effective and non-representational unity on which the possibility of remembrance rests."[65] He means to say that our whole possible experience, which includes also our past, is encapsulated in it. Evidently, he is inviting us to a withdrawal to the vicinity of Being and by the same token to the divine level. For he is fully aware that-- to put it in his own words--:"To withdraw into oneself

is not to be for oneself nor to mirror oneself in the
intelligible unity of subject and object." We are still
on a deeper level, he warns us; for he goes on to add:
"On the contrary, I would say that here we come up
against the actual mystery whereby the I into which I
withdraw ceases, for as much, to belong to itself. `You
are not your own'--this great saying of St. Paul assumes
in this connection its full concrete and ontological
significance; it is the nearest approach to the reality
for which we are groping."[66] And yet, as it was recently openly acknowledged by the participants in a panel
discussion as reported in Entretiens autour de Gabriel
Marcel,[67] he is not inviting us to a genuine mystical
experience, which he himself never enjoyed. He remains
anchored to the philosophical shore and he is speaking
solely of our human cognitive powers and of the ordinary
manifestations of Being. As to the former, he warns us
that it is not properly an intuition, or, at least, not
an ordinary intuition, but an illuminating, unobjectif-
iable one. "The more an intuition is central and basic
in the being whom it illuminates," he writes, "the less
it is capable of turning back and apprehending itself."[68] At this point it would seem that he does not
find the right words, for he goes on: "We are here at
the most difficult point of our whole discussion.
Rather than to speak of intuition in this context, we
should say that we are dealing with an assurance which
underlies the entire development of thought, even of
discursive thought."[69] If therefore the validity of the
conclusions reached by our ordinary reflection--by our
"primary reflection," to use his own formula-- is to be
established, we must bring about the thread that binds
them with this underlying ultimate and unique foundation
of truth, which, as he puts it, "can therefore be

approached only by a second reflection--a reflection whereby I ask myself how and from what starting point I was able to proceed in my initial reflection, which itself postulated the ontological, but without knowing it."[70] In other words, in its purest essence it is an inquiry into the conditions of possibility of whatever we know by using the very demanding principle of sufficient reason, the pressing demands of which in "the entire development of thought" are themselves directly prompted by the blind intuition itself. In this sense recollection cannot be separated from second reflection. Marcel could even say: "This second reflection is recollection in the measure in which recollection can be self-conscious."[71]

At this point it is easy to recognize in the blind intuition and its attached "recollection" what ultimately accounts for Marcel's writings as a whole. For his concrete philosophy comes down to the best response to the illness hat Heidegger had diagnosed so well but could never cure: "Upon reflection"--he writes in En chemin vers quel éveil?--"it is there that my essential agreement with Heidegger on what he has called the oblivion of Being seems to become more apparent to me."[72] That this concern really does constitute his ultimate reality and meaning becomes an inescapable conclusion through the following relatively recent confession: "If any sense of direction did in fact guide my work, it is indeed the persistent effort that I always displayed during the last sixty years to hem as much as possible the abyss that so many spirits skirt in an appalling state of blindness."[73] With Marcel, therefore, "It may be said in this respect that no concrete philosophy is possible without a constantly renewed yet creative tension between the I and those depths of our being in and by which we are; nor without the most stringent and rigorous reflection, directed on our most intensely lived experience."[74]

This leads us back to the mysterious "object" of the blinded intuition which, as a submerged Atlantis, teases us by surfacing and sneaking out in different forms here and there at certain landmarks of our life, but never long enough to let itself be observed as an object. Under the circumstances, therefore, we can repeat with Marcel: "If we now consider being as something inexhaustibly concrete, we will note first that it cannot function as a datum, properly speaking, that it cannot be observed but only acknowledged--I am even tempted to say, if the term did not have a foreign ring to the philosophical ear--not so much acknowledged as greeted."[75] And yet, its silent presence is not thereby rendered any less effective. Despite its different metamorphoses--musical, poetical, moral, and even technological--, it is always the same presence that emerges and it always leaves a creating impact. Marcel puts it in a very inspired way; he describes those peak moments of our life that we call "creative" as follows: "The same presence and the same appeal to the soul by the Being within it can be found in any creative act whether visible or not; the act, the same with itself despite the inexhaustibility of its manifestations, testifies to this same presence, and the soul can challenge or annul it insofar as it is a soul endowed with freedom."[76]

Human existence is therefore an ongoing and dramatic dialogue between Being and us, between Being exhorting us through our own nature to reach a perfect and joyful possession of itself, and us, humans, either wisely giving our consent by trusting the ontological direction of our own "Being," or blindly thrusting ourselves into the worldly spree of "Having," desparately trying to hold on to the riches provided by technology while completely overlooking the wealth of Being that lies inside ourselves. Existing, in other words, starts always at a crossroads, where we are given a choice between Having and Being, between the way of mystery and the problematical attitude. In this decision-making process, recollection corresponds to the recognition of the mystery of participation, the only approach to which "is quite the contrary of that demanded by the solution of a problem." Indeed, he goes on to add: "to solve a problem, the mind must turn outside itself, it must fling itself on the elements with which it must work. One should add that this inner grasp or grip"--he explains, referring to the right attitude--"seems always to have the aspect of an easing of tension, of a letting go, and not of a willed tensing-up of oneself."77 Perhaps we ought to go further and say that it is a humble surrender to the appeal of Being, which in cognitive terms amounts to the antithesis of an hyper-critical frame of mind--far from an indolent "state of relaxedness," though -- and is guaranteed by the assurance provided by blinded intuition; and in moral terms leads straight to love. Indeed, since participation makes us "co-present" to any being in whom Being affirms itself, this surrender to Being in our Being ultimately means disposability to others and finally to the absolute Thou. For, on the one hand, "co-presence," which entailscompenetration and co-sharing, must be free of the ideas of "indifference" and "indisposability," which

in turn are implied by bare "co-existence" to the extent
that the latter entails exteriority and therefore lack
of solicitude. This can easily be seen in the way two
trees coexist with one another for years. So Marcel
says: "Co-presence cannot be expressed in terms of co-
existence;" and on the other hand, as he puts it: "The
more non-disposable I am, the more will God appear to me
as `someone who.' And that is just a denial of co-
presence."78

In the following passage, which summarizes Marcel's
warnings against what he calls the Philosophy of the
But, the inward trend of recollection is better
explained by contrast: "we must have lost touch with the
fundamental truth that knowledge implies a previous
askesis-purification, in fact-- and that when all is
said and done, knowledge in its fullness is not vouch-
safed except where it has first been deserved. And here
once more I think that the progress of applied science,
and the habit of considering knowledge itself as a
technical operation which leaves the knower wholly unaf-
fected, has powerfully militated against a clear view of
these matters. The askesis or purification must chiefly
lie, it is clear, in progressively detaching ourselves
from speculative thought in so far as it is purely
critical and simply the faculty of making objections."79
Without recollection, for one thing, our approach to
Marcel's references to St. John's Gospel would be utterly impossible.

footnotes

[1]Jeanne Delhomme, "Le jugement en `je'," in <u>Revue</u> <u>de</u> <u>Métaphysique</u> <u>et</u> <u>de</u> <u>Morale</u>, 79 (1974), p. 292.

[2]See Peccorini, <u>O.c.</u>, pp. 184-187.

[3]Willard Van Orman Quine, <u>Word</u> <u>and</u> <u>Object</u> (Cambridge, MA.: The MIT Press, 1960), p. 59.

[4]<u>MJ</u>, p. 2.

[5]<u>O.c.</u>, p. 1.

[6]See Peccorini, <u>On</u> <u>to</u> <u>the</u> <u>World</u> <u>of</u> <u>Freedom</u>, p. 187.

[7]<u>Mj</u>, p. 42.

[8]<u>O.c.</u>, pp. 42-43.

[9]<u>O.c.</u>, p. 43.

[10]<u>Ibid</u>.

[11]<u>Ibid</u>.

[12]<u>O.c.</u>, p. 44.

[13]<u>Ibid</u>.

[14]<u>O.c.</u>, p. 67.

[15]<u>O.c.</u>, p. 44.

[16]<u>Ibid</u>.

[17] O.c., p. 45.

[18] Ibid.

[19] O.c., p. 46.

[20] O.c., pp. 61-62.

[21] See Gabriel Marcel interrogé par Pierre Boutang, 1977, pp. 70-71.

[22] CrF, p. 30.

[23] PhFr, p. 82.

[24] PhEx, p. 25.

[25] MJ, p. 45.

[26] Ibid.

[27] Ibid.

[28] Ibid.

[29] O.c., p. 70.

[30] O.c., p. 68.

[31] O.c., p. 69.

[32] O.c., pp. 41-42.

[33] O.c., p. 42.

[34] Ibid.

[35] O.c., p. 181.

[36] Ibid.

[37] O.c., p. 183.

[38] Ibid.

[39] O.c., p. 184.

[40] O.c., p. 186.

[41] O.c., p. 184.

[42] Ibid. See also pp. 220-221; Marcel, BH, pp. 76-82.

[43] PhEx, p. 14.

[44] MJ, pp. 185-186.. See also BH, p. 167 and p. 149, note.

[45] MJ, p. 186.

[46] O.c., p. 58. See also the end of p. 57. See MB, II, pp. 68-69.

[47] See Searchings, p. 42.

[48] MJ, pp. 184-185.

[49] MJ, pp. 62-63. See BH, p. 212.

[50] MJ, p. 64. See also pp. 221-222.

[51] PhEx, p. 49.

[52] Ibid.

[53] CrF, p. 162.

[54] O.c., p. 164.

[55] BH, p. 69.

[56] CrF, p. 167.

[57] EBHE, p. 169.

[58]O.c., pp. 133-134.

[59]TrW, pp. 113-115; MB, II, pp. 132-133.

[60]BH, p. 72.

[61]CrF, p. 167.

[62]Ibid.

[63]See Marcel, "Existentialisme et pensée chrétienne," in Témoignages, 5 (1947), p. 165. See also BH, pp. 111-112.

[64]BH, pp. 120-121.

[65]PhEx, p. 24.

[66]O.c., pp. 24-25.

[67]See: Entretiens autour de Gabriel Marcel, p. 225.

[68]PhEx, p. 25.

[69]Ibid.

[70]Ibid.

[71]Ibid.

[72]EChE, 1971, p. 202.

[73]O.c., p. 203.

[74]CrF, p. 65.

[75]O.c., p. 69. See also p. 138.

[76]O.c., p. 10.

[77]Man Against Mass Society [MAMS], 1962, pp. 91-92.

[78]BH, p. 81.

[79]O.c., p. 190.

Chapter IV

The Roots of the Human Community in
"The Light of Christ"

Obviously, the type of specific communication through love is based on intersubjectivity, which is real despite its not being "objective" in the sense of empirical. Marcel, on the other hand, does not ignore that intersubjectivity is not a familiar concept for the positivists whom he is bent upon enlightening. For it is not any kind of physical interaction that should be understood in terms of wave-transmissions. Essentially it is an "openness" of one to another, the implications of which are not accessible to anyone who is totally alien to the philosophy of light which lately--perhaps since 1971--had become a kind of philosophico-religious obsession on Marcel's part.

1 - Intersubjectivity Through the Light of Christ.

That new approach to Being might be described also as working on the only givenness of Being that he was willing to accept after those ontological puzzles that he had just gone through during the exposé of the Question of Being.[1] That such was his final position became clear in the discussion that ensued upon the closing of that exposé and during which Mr. Gaston Berger--after so many groping efforts on the part of the other panelists--managed to put his finger on. What ought to stop Marcel's questions and the flux of his endless--shall we say?--"cavillings" about Being by distinguishing three states for the latter: (1) the original givenness of Being which is beyond our grasp-- Marcel calls it participation and says that it can only be "retrieved" through a second reflection--, (2) the manifestation of that givenness, which corresponds to what Marcel calls the blinded intuition, and finally (3) the fullness of Being, which is only found in God. Insofar as it is given to us solely in blinded intuition, Being sheds much light on our existential steps by encompassing all of them under the question of Being and thereby determining the meaning of human existence as to its general upward direction.

That is what Gaston Berger calls the "itinerant thinking," which he labels "the most important activity of the spirit in the interval which is actually being traversed." "Thus," he writes, "it seems to me that in your thought there is a kind of option offered between being, which would immediately be realized or given, and an existence which is in search of itself through a personal journey in which the emphasis is precisely on questioning. What is given is the question, even before it is known who is questioning, who must respond, and what the question is about; even before it is known what kind of satisfaction the question is going to provide."[2]

No wonder that such a marvelous summary of Gabriel Marcel's thought immediately prompted the philosopher to comment: "You have expressed my thought admirably, probably much better than I have done."[3] And indeed, in Présence et immortalité Marcel himself had stressed the blind alley of human itinerant thinking which is going towards God but does go unwittingly, as it were, unless either revelation comes along or the philosophical second reflection follows suit. In his view the latter, as a matter of fact, is enough, as he tells us while referring to the implications of that "openness" of one to another and to the whole of reality that he had mentioned a few lines before. He even goes on to say: "I think that the latter [the implications of openness] cannot be extricated if it is not through a philosophy of light,"[4] not without warning us that, although he means by light something very close to what St. John had in mind in the preface to his own Gospel, he does not have to resort to Revelation to carry out such an extrication. In an effort to be more specific he adds: "For instance, one might perfectly well speak of the light of knowledge, and I should even add that one must do so: otherwise the very epistemology itself would dry out and be denatured."[5]

There is no doubt therefore that the light whose free flow must be guaranteed[6] is the light that constitutes the "pensée pensante;" it is the light that comes from Being although the moment and the act of its emergence from the latter escapes our grasp.[7] Marcel leaves no room for doubt in that respect, and he even anticipates what Mr. Gaston Berger just told us a while ago: "I insisted on the importance of what I called `concrete approaches.' We cannot, I think, install ourselves in being itself, we cannot capture it or seize it, any more than we can see the source giving off light––all we can see are surfaces illuminated by the light. I think that this comparison between being and light is a fundamental one. And I hardly need mention that at this point I am very close to the Gospel of John where he speaks of the

`Light which lighteth every man that cometh into the
world.'8 Indeed Marcel fully realizes that John himself
is speaking of the Word understood also precisely and
exclusively in his capacity as an ontological foundation
for the human existence of all men, regardless of their
having faith or not--which is why the Gospel can most
categorically refer to "every man who cometh into the
world" thereby leaving out the formal incorporation into
the mystical body--; this being the reason why he
accordingly adds: "to be a human being would be to
participate in this light, while failing to do so would
mean sinking to the level of the animal or lower
still."9

Antonio Rosmini echoes Marcel, but at the same time
he explains the "naturalness" of the light. "Under
natural conditions"--he wrote in his prologue to the
Gospel according to John--"man is granted the idea of
Being in general, but not divine subsistence in its
self-manifestation." He then pointed out that man "is
not given the Word either, but only a light coming forth
from the Word. From the point of view of man, therefore," he concluded, "the self-manifesting Being gets so
diminished and curtailed that it is reduced to the size
of a simple Idea or concept of Being without subsistence. In the process, of course, the notions of God and
Word get lost to the extent that the Word and God do not
bear the least limitation."10

Consequently, Marcel can remind us at the end of
that chapter that it is not any kind of intuition of
Being that triggers our whole process of knowledge and
love--of humanity, as he just surmised--, but that sense
of security that constantly recurs in his writings and

that he called "blinded intuition. " He pointed out too
that such a blinded intuition is so conceptually incon-
spicuous that it is to be retrieved by means of a second
reflection, namely, through a "reflection which dwells
on being, depending not on an intuition but on an assurance identical with what we call our soul."[11] It is
that wonderful blinded intuition, which is both
illumining and humanizing and does away with frontiers
of all sorts between me and the others as well as
between the object and the subject, that is to be
retrieved through second reflection if we want to understand the mystery of intersubjectivity.

This places us in a milieux where Being shows up in
different forms and flows freely in all directions. "I
am thinking"--says Marcel in Présence et immortalité --
"of creation, and particularly of dramatic and musical
creations. And it is enough to bring to mind the way in
which a melodic idea arises: it simply happens, it takes
over our minds. Where does it come from? Does it
originate in me or somewhere else? But upon reflection
it immediately becomes clear that such a distinction is
absolutely meaningless in this connection."[12] Only for
the idealists are there borderlines, and this is so
because idealism really needs such a myth as the only
possible foundation for its monadism. Marcel has strong
words against those who, based on such grounds, object
to realities such as telepathy and other phenomena of
the kind, even though the latter have been scientifical-
ly verified. On his part, he rather sees in them a
confirmation of the metaphysical intersubjectivity that
makes up the core of his philosophy. "Here"--he says,
speaking of the telepathic experiences--"takes place a
sort of confluence between the metapsychical experiences

and an autonomous reflection which from the speculative
point of view is bound to cast doubts on the whole post-
Cartesian philosophy to the extent that the latter
zeroes in on the Cogito understood in a restrictive
sense--whereas the critique of the "I" (moi, je...)
cannot help but open for us the doors of a liberating
metaphysics."13

2 - Marcel's Anti-Cartesian Aristotelianism.

It is refreshing to hear Marcel qualify his
personal position as being essentially "anti-Cartesian"
because this allows us to look upon his "intersubjectivity" in terms of the Aristotelian ontologically
"totalizing" characteristics of both the possible
intellect--which can become "all things"--and the agent
mind--which can accordingly make "all things"-- a characteristic at that which gives the mind a truly
"liberating" and infinitely "expanding" powers-; and we
are indeed allowed to do so because it is precisely
Aristotle's incompatibility with the essence of
Cartesianism that Marcel mentioned to Pierre Boutang in
1977 as the reason for his own "Aristotelianism," and
because such an "anti-Cartesianism" was defined by him
precisely in terms of "openness" and "liberation"--a
liberation in which even the body is called upon to take
part.

Indeed, he had just stated that in his philosophy,
the body, far from barring the drive towards universality that our soul experiences, works on the same level
with the mind with which it cooperates by opening the
gates of the external world. "That was for me"--he says
alluding to the body's immediacy that is dealt with in

the Metaphysical Journal -- "a kind of discovery towards
the end of 1929. It suddenly became clear to me that if
I could truly get in touch with the world it was because
of this non-objectifiable character which is proper to
my body and that I feel." And it was precisely at that
point that Boutang cut with the following transcendental
question: "Did by chance Aristotle's Treatise on the
Soul ever appear to you as leading to what you have just
said?" Marcel snapped at once an answer which is a
jewel within our context: "Possibly, for the last time
that I went over Aristotle's philosophy--ancient history
indeed since it was at Montpellier during the 1940 war--
I had the feeling that his philosophy was after all far
closer to mine than I had ever realized. For sure,
whatever anti-Cartesianism--forgive the anachronism--
there is in Aristotle's thought is very similar to my
thought."14

As a parenthesis we might volunteer the following
Aristotelian account of the body's intervention which
would parallel--in more technical terms, of course--the
existential hints dropped by Marcel here and there.
Sensibility, which is the faculty by means of which the
soul informs the body, contains the actuality of all
material things that there may be in the universe at all
times, and it does so--it "is" such an actuality, we
might say--from birth. This is the reason why Aristotle
does not require an agent sense. As the soul is already
and always all material things through sensibility,15
all that is needed for sensation to happen is the impact
from the outside object, which is already "actually
sensible." Upon the latter's happening the object
immediately appears with its own Being literally
emerging from the actualization that sensibility has

just gone through under the physical impact. Since that impact is physical, it is not absurd to consider the possibility of certain organisms being specially fitted to be impacted by very special kinds of waves that would permit distant objects to make their impact felt from afar as it is supposed to happen in cases of extra-sensory perception. This would seem to confirm Marcel's conjectures on the clairvoyant's powers.[16]

Based precisely on the same insight, St. Thomas Aquinas could also build up his theory of the emanation of the faculties from the substance of the soul wherein sensibility emanates from the Being of the self through the possible intellect and is ordained altogether to the service of the latter.[17] When death arrives, that power is no longer exercised because it is no longer needed; and yet, as long as its principle lies in the soul's substance--which remains for ever--one might say that according to Aquinas we take with us to the afterlife a virtual body which can account for the possibility of resurrection.[18] On the other hand, since the feeling of my body as mine is a "vital" phenomenon and must therefore be traced directly to the ongoing actual information of the body by the soul, we might well say that what we feel is ourselves living through our sens-ible faculty, which virtually remains in its principle even after our death. In the Entretiens autour de Gabriel Marcel that took place in 1976 there is a reply given by Marcel to René Poirier that seems to assume the foregoing as a premise.

In reference to his having left behind Descartes' dualism, Marcel says: "There is therefore a certain perspective from which it can be said that the body survives. This, in turn, leads me to give you an answer, which will be quite precise and, this time, even categorical, to your question concerning resurrection. In my view," he goes on to say keeping his mind on the body-object, which is nothing but the material organism that can be sensed and manipulated as any other object-- "it is quite evident that it is indeed the resurrection of the flesh that is at stake, but by that it is not the resurrection of the body-object that is meant."[19] We might even add that finally in 1973, under the persistent and guiding questioning to which he was subjected by his dear friend and excellent interpreter, Mrs. Parain-Vial, he unequivocally acknowledged the Aristotelian foundation of this position.[20]

All things considered, therefore, the least we can say is that it would be unreasonable to doubt of the identity between the Marcellian philosophy of "Light" and the Aristotelian doctrine on the light of Being, which coming down through the agent intellect finally trickles down to sensibility thereby enabling it to take part in the knowing process. Jeanne Parain-Vial brings to our attention a passage coined by Marcel in 1969 that tends to buttress that impression, with the advantage of showing also how in Marcel's mind that light links us with one another through our innermost constituent, thereby giving rise to the sense of community to which love is essential as a foundation: "In my thought," he wrote in Revue de Métaphysique et de Morale (p. 256,n.3,1969)--"the essences, as I think I mentioned it somewhere, are the modalities of the Light that, speaking in St. John's terms, enlightens all men who come into this world; it should be added too that the light that is at stake is a Light which is a joy of being

Light. Now, if we try to extricate the implications contained in this formula, it becomes clear that this light presupposes an indefinite multitude of beings to which it gives rise in view of two purposes, namely, in order to illumine them and also so that they in turn may illumine others."[21]

The relation between Being as Light and the joy of being Light, which Marcel has just pointed to, cannot help but connote the fact that Being as Light is no other than Being as the infinite subject, and since such an infinite subject cannot pursue any other goal in whatever he does and produces but the glory of his beloved goodness, it is easy to understand why behaving as light causes him such joy. Consequently, it makes full sense that no finite subject, in his capacity as a participation in Light, will ever be able to have another natural destiny but to love and glorify the divine Being. Hence, enjoying the fact of being an irradiating center of Light obviously points in the direction of love's being as much an essential manifest-ation of our ontological and constitutive participation as our cognitive potentials have already been acknow-ledged to be. Furthermore, the fact, also mentioned by Marcel, that Being constitutes us into persons so that wetoomay love it and enable others to do the same is a clear indication that according to him human perfection cannot do without our love for God.[22]

3 - The Christ as the Foundation of the Community.

It is therefore the Light of God that ultimately

unites virtuous persons. Marcel, at least, could not find any better explanation for what his encounter with the heroic young priest of Dresde, Siegfried Foelz, meant to him: "Indeed"--he wrote-- "it was as though not I only had been given the power to apperceive a certain light, but simultaneously I had suddenly been assured that the same light was currently being seen by the other, the brother who was both distant and by my side."[23] Sciacca, by simply substituting for the word (light) the term (presence) fully corroborates the fact: "He who communicates with himself and with the others in the strongest and most meaningful sense of the word must be in God's presence; furthermore, he does in fact fully realize that he is rooted in and tightly tied up to that presence."[24]

This, of course, sheds much light on Marcel's conversion to the Catholic Church. It is well known that it was Christ as Light that remained for ever the only reason for his faithfulness to the Mystical Body. In 1976 he wrote in what was meant to be his testament the following eloquent words: "The light of Christ: upon articulating those words I feel a strange emotion. The reason for this is that such words mean something unusual, they mean that for my spirit Christ is not as much an object on which I could concentrate my attention as an irradiating center of Light which can also become a look. But, as a look he cannot be looked at, he can only penetrate us and, perhaps, all the more so to the extent that one feels oneself the object of his look."[25]

Such a tenderness towards Christ suggests that the light that constitutes all human persons not only con- stitutes the divine persons all the more; it also makes

them the object of the fullness of our loving power
without the saturation of which our perfection would be
unattainable. In other words, it makes God's presence
necessary for our Being. But, by the same token this
love for Christ--an echo of St. Paul's longings--
literally "demands" Marcel's immortality. This consequence is clearly stated through the following
quotation: "But, it is well understood, the nexus from
which this demand arises can only be love, not I do not
know what unbridled will to live. Indeed, such is the
reason why this demand can and must be looked upon as
irresistible and unstpppable."26 In other words, this
demand of immortality is an argument for immortality
since God's eternal possession is presented as necessary
for my Being.

It is this nexus or consequence, therefore, that is
to be well established. For one thing, as it is going
to be shown in the following chapter on the basis of our
ability to transcend the chemical processes of life
through the experience of "presence," immortality is
possible. On the other hand, it has just been made
clear that it is also necessary for human beings. Now,
if we view both of these conclusions in the light of the
premises established in Chapter II, section 3 of this
book, we will have a fully polished argument for
immortality. Indeed, when we were concerned with
certainty and ontological appetite, we came to the
conclusion that whatever is indispensable for the
spiritual growth of our own Being is true and that
therefore just as our faith in it is infallible our
willing it cannot be subject to the modality of
possibility.27 As we remember, Marcel would go as far
as to say that "to will is to affirm: `I depend on that

(I will only be if that is), hence that depends on me.'28 And he would reinforce that position with the following mind-boggling statement:"...I can only have faith in what I am or, to be more exact, in that by which I am. I mean that faith could not have bearing on a metaphysical order that was radically foreign to me..."29

In Marcel's opinion it was precisely the lack of this insight into the ontological demands of man's constitution that prevented Heidegger from taking the leap of faith in God. He said this in the final paragraph of a study on the German philosopher. He wrote: "...Heidegger has the very great merit of recognizing the intimate bond that links Being and the Sacred. But I am afraid that, due to his lack of understanding of both the neighbor as a person and intersubjectivity, it is impossible for him to enter the sphere where the family resemblance--if not the identity--between Being and the Sacred finds its full and rewarding significance."30

This argument based on the modality of necessity takes on a more Marcellian flavor when referred to the presence of the beloved one who has died. As he explained during his South American tour of 1951, quoting from his Mystère de l'être (I,pp.220-221): "But through a reverse phenomenon it may occur that the other will in fact cause an internal renewal in myself if I come to feel his presence: such a presence is thereby made a revealing presence, and that means that it makes me be more fully than I would be without it."31 In this sense, he goes on to say to his South American audiences, this experience is strictly speaking an existential one, for "it is not so much what the other says, or the content of his words, that exerts on me such a stimulating influence; it is the fact that he himself is saying them, that he is backing them up with the whole of his Being."32 Marcel insists on the fact that such a presence is real, personal, and in no way a matter of special effects due to an acting technique that could be learned and used in order to promote a campaign of public relations. It is the other's presence that has become an indispensable factor in my personal growth. On the basis of the foregoing premises therefore the following declarations cannot sound unwarranted, all the more so that he contrasts them with the mere conjectural "hypothesis" that we might build up on the basis of mere psychic experiences combined with the principle of sufficient reason. "Now," he writes to introduce the antithesis, "the presence as I evoked it is supra-hypothetical and gives rise to an invincible assurance which is linked to the self-giving love (amour oblatif) and finds expression in statements such as these: ˋI am sure that you remain present to me and such a certainty is based on the fact that you keep on assisting me, that you assist me perhaps more directly now than you could do it while you were on earth. We are together within the light, or more exactly, when I detach myself from myself and stop shedding my shadow on myself, I enter a light which is your light; and I do not mean by that the light of which you are the source, but rather that one in which you are blooming and that you reflect and irradiate on me."33

Evidently, the metaphor of Light has brought us all the way to a universal community which is also eternal.

footnotes

1See TrW, pp. 45-80.

2O.c., p. 78.

3O.c., p. 79.

4Présence et immortalité, [PI], 1959, p. 189.

5Ibid.

6CrF, p. 13.

7MB, II, p. 35; TrW, pp. 48-49.

8TrW, p. 14.

9Ibid.

10See L'introduzione al Vangelo di S. Giovanni, Ediz. Nz., p. 31. For a better understanding of the distincion see Peccorini, F.L., From Gentile's "Actualism" to Sciacca's "Idea." Beyond Existentialism and Phenomenology Towards the Philosophy of Integrality (Genoa: Studio Editoriale de Cultura; Arlington, VA: Carrollton Press Inc., 1981. Currently being distributed by The University Publications of America, Frederick, Maryland), p. 60. See also Santino Cavaciuti, Momenti della ontologia contemporanea. M.Blondel, L. Lavelle, M.F. Sciacca (Roma: cittá Nuova Ed., 1976), p. 353 and Il pensiero de Etienne Vacherot, (Lucca: Ed. del Testimone, 1976), pp. 182-185, 187-191.

11TrW, p. 15. See also John Francis Quinn, The

Historical Constitution of St. Bonaventure's
Philosophy (Toronto: Pontifical Institute of
Medieval Studies, 1973), pp. 528-529.

12PI, p. 190.

13O.c., p. 191.

14Gabriel Marcel interrogé par Pierre Boutang, pp.
75-76.

15See Aristotle, De Anima, 417b16-19 and 431b20-
432a10.

16Marcel, MJ, pp. 270-271.

17See S.Th, I, 77,6, ad 3m. See also Peccorini,
From Gentile's "Actualism" to Sciacca's "Idea", pp.
83-84.

18See S.Th., I, 77,8 in c.

19Entretiens autour de Gabriel Marcel, p. 169. See
The Existential Background of Human Dignity [EBHE],
1963, p. 46.

20"Dialogues entre G. Marcel et Mme. Parain-Vial,"
1974, pp. 388-391.

21Entretiens autour de Gabriel Marcel, p. 201.

22Homo Viator [HV], 1944, p. 152.

23EChE, 1971, p. 251.

24Michele Federico Sciacca,Interiorità Oggettiva
(Milan: Marzorati Editore, 1967), p. 111; see
Peccorini, From Gentile's "Actualism"..., p. 172,
and Marcel, MB, II, pp. 12-13. See also
Troisfontaines, "Le mystère de la mmort," in Revue
de Met. et de Morale, 79 (1974), p. 333.

25EChE, p. 287. See TrW, p. 243.

[26]EChE, p. 286.

[27]MB, II, pp. 68-69.

[28]MJ, pp. 185-186.

[29]MJ, p. 186.

[30]Gabriel Marcel et la pensée allemande, 1979, p. 38; see also TrW, p. 131.

[31]PI, p. 188.

[32]Ibid.

[33]O.c., p. 191.

Chapter V

Immortality and Love

In 1937, during the International Philosophical
Convention held in Paris, Leon Brunschvicg--the bril-
liant idealist philosopher who had been Marcel's
Professor at the Sorbonne--, commenting on his former
student's paper said "that the death of Gabriel Marcel
seemed to preoccupy Gabriel Marcel more than the death
of Leon Brunschvicg preoccupied Leon Brunschvicg;" and
we know that Marcel snapped back immediately centering
the question of immortality by calling the audience's
attention to the fact that Brunschvicg "had posed the
question very badly." Then he went on to add: "the only
thing worth preoccupying either one of us was the death
of someone we loved."[1]

Marcel, for sure, was not stepping over any new
ground. In fact, as he had confided many times in the
past and did confide most emphatically once more to
Pierre Boutang before his own death, when his beloved
mother died he swore that he would someday find out all
about immortality. "I think"--he told Boutang--"that it
is impossible to exaggerate the importance that my
mother's death had in my life. It is a fact that a few
years later, walking on one of the lanes of the Monceau
Park which is still vividly present to my imagination, I
inquired from my aunt if one could ever know what was
the fate of those we call `the dead ones.' Upon hearing
her response to the effect that unfortunately there was

no way to know, I replied--as I remember-- with a somehow childish pretentiousness: `Well, later on I will try
to understand'."2

1 - Away From Heidegger On His Way to Immortality.

In this light, it is easy to understand how petty
an approach it would be in Marcel's opinion to consider
death as a mere biological fact or even as an idea-- as
though it were possible for anyone to get rid of death
just as one gets rid of an idea, a point he had made
before in the paper that he presented to the 1937
philosophical convention held in Paris.[3] His approach
was rather oriented from the outset towards the relation
of death to Freedom. He tried to establish death's
counterpoise, and after having eliminated life--which
after all is connoted by death--and any kind of objective truth, as we saw him doing in the preceding
paragraph, he settled for a positive use of Freedom
through which Freedom supposedly rejects "the pernicious
self-deception that induces life to transfer to death a
power that it alone has a right to use." As a result he
was led to conclude: "Freedom then acquires a new
meaning: it becomes an affirmation and love; and death
is thus transcended."[4]

The new picture we see is that of life affirming
itself through love, and that means Being--insofar as it
knows and loves itself in and through any human person--
freely affirming itself in the act of faith which lies
at the foundation of man's existence--and even of
logic--, and thereby loving itself in all its forms and
in all selves. Indeed, the implication of love is what

Marcel misses most in Heigegger's approach, as he often made very clear. None less than the tight case he made against the Heideggerian position ended in that somber note. "These remarks"--he wrote then--"lead to a recognition of something basic which Heidegger has in no way suspected because, despite appearances, he reminds the prisoner not of a theoretical but of an existential solipsism. (I would say almost the same for Sartre)." And undoubtedly what was missing in those philosophers' approach was the lack of focus on the death of the beloved one, "the fact that, most profoundly, the consideration of one's own death is surpassed by the consideration of the death of a loved one."5

This accusation of lack of concern for love and intersubjectivity was his main and decisive criticism against Heidegger. He even dared to accuse the German philosopher of this shortcoming in the latter's own fatherland. Speaking of that gap between himself and the Teutonic, he added: "One of those differences bears almost certainly on the very notion of intersubjectivity. Indeed, it is impossible to pinpoint in the doctrine exposed in `Sein und Zeit' anything that remotely resembles solipsism. Beyond any doubt, Being-in-the World bespeaks a certain plurality-- of what? of subjects? I am not quite sure of the latter. But, to me Heidegger, who spoke so often of Erschlossenheit or of Entfernung in connection with truth, never showed the least interest in what we might call the `openness to the other' or more concretely to love. It is this dimension that the psychiatrist and philosopher Binswanger could not help but miss in the elechus of Heideggerian categories and made up for so unfortunate an omission by adding it on his own in his great work,

Grundformen und Erkenntnis des menschlichen Daseins
(Niehans, Zurich, 1942)."[6]

Another criticism, on which he insisted with zest,
was concerned with Heidegger's faulty language. But,
having to do with another philosopher's position
exclusively, it is completely tangential to his own
belief in immortality. With a touch of irony, commenting on the sense of achievement of which Heidegger--
unwarrantedly, of course, in Marcel's opinion--had bragged upon his allegedly having improved the approach to
existence, the French philosopher rejected the implied
concept of Dasein both on linguistic grounds and from an
existential point of view. "The earlier interpretation,
which was based on ordinary everydayness," he remarked,
"was limited to the analysis of existing indifferently,
that is, inauthentically. But in this respect there was
something essential missing in this ontological characterization of the structure of existence." Then he
goes on to wonder: "What sort of lack was it, if not
with respect to this totality which has just been evoked
-- and which cannot be understood without placing death
as its terminal brick."[7] Marcel could therefore conclude in the following terms: "So it is a question of
highlighting Dasein's completedness, and consequently,
rather than considering Dasein's position midway between
life and death, considering instead the end, das Ende."[8]

Marcel cannot help but read in this new approach a
questionable built-in concept of existence that must
serve as a criterion for the Ganzheit which is being
contemplated, and that concept, says Marcel, comes down
to death viewed from the point of view of the Dasein as
the latter's "existentielle" Sein zum Tod.

Marcel rejects this new concept on the grounds that it makes death essential to the completion of human Being, and that it does so on the basis of a vague terminology. He grants that this would be true if, and only if, in the formula Sein zum Tod the word "zu" stood for the preposition "for." The implication is that it cannot stand for "towards" because "towards" calls for a verb of motion, which the verb "to be" certainly is not.[9] But if it means "for," Sein zum Tod turns out to convey either one of the following ideas: "Etre pour la mort can mean être livré à la mort [to be delivered to death], but also être destiné à mourir [to be destined to die], or être condamné à mourir [to be condemned to die]."[10] Marcel prefers version number two but he finds that it does not fit in Heidegger's thought precisely to the extent that it implies finality: "Fidelity to Heidegger's thinking," he says, "to the degree that his thought can be comprehended, requires, I think, removing completely the notion of finality from the word pour. But it is impossible to use the words `destined to' without preserving some tint of finality."[11] However, even if it did, he seems to be saying that the way to establish such a finality would be problematic. For it cannot be established through logical deduction. In this connection he asks himself: "Do I have grounds for saying that the `must die' is truly implied by being-in-the world? I could, it is true, construct for myself an a posteriori account to the effect that my being-in-the-world is assured by mechanical functions which, just because they are mechanisms, cannot function perpet-ually...But there is a catch. The argument presupposes that I can detach myself sufficiently from my being-in-the-world to substitute for it something else, which would first have to have been divested of what I would readily call its experiential weight."12 In other words, we cannot obtain a Sein zum Tod through logical deduction unless we borrow our premises from an experience that is not human. Furthermore, in Marcel's view we cannot make death essential to the completion of human Being if we only use our human experience. He puts it rather bluntly: "Death cannot even be called an end--which Heidegger himself seems to recognize from time to time, but not without contradicting himself. For example, he says that in death Dasein is neither accomplished nor has simply disappeared nor has terminated nor has become manageable (Verfügbar) again like something at hand (Zuhandenen). I think that death appears as an end only when life is seen as a kind of journey. But life appears this way only when I consider it from outside--and to the degree I consider it this way, I no longer experience life as my life."13 This thought finds its explanation in what he had written before in Creative Fidelity: "...I can overcome death by imagining it as already come full term only on condition of putting myself in someone else's place, someone who will survive me and who will experience my death as if it were his death."14 Obviously, he does not recognize his own experience in that garb. His own experience rather sides with Spinoza's testimony, for which he finds the best support in men's experience at large: "Perhaps"--he writes--"this having to die is immediately apprehended, not inferred, so that I would have to avow that I perceive or experience myself as mortal, as having to die. But here again we meet Spinoza. Spinoza affirms that we perceive and experience ourselves as immortal. All our experiences of fullness, experiences like love, creation, and contemplation, where we are aware of attaining being, testify in Spinoza's behalf."15

If there is something that Marcel never agreed about with Heidegger it certainly was the latter's use of the formula Sein zum Tod. He maintained his opposition until his death. Still in August of 1973, when he met with his friends at the age of 84 to review his own philosophy at the Cerisy-La-Salle Castle, he had the opportunity to say it to the whole world with the strongest possible words. Not even Paul Ricoeur's remark that Heidegger did not place his treatise on Sein zum Tod within the framework of the in-der-Welt-Sein, but rather within the treatment of the care, the temporal structure of which it was meant to bring about through the complete reciprocity between the past, the present and the future, could shake his conviction. He snapped a rather angry reply to it that undoubtedly was prompted in part by his suddenly having remembered the senseless death of a young man who died in a train derailment despite the fact that he had had the opportunity to travel by car: "I protest most strongly"--he said--"against that sort of professorial oversimplification that seems to me totally out of tune with the positions of a human existence. I cannot stand it and what you have just said cannot help but stiffen my fundamental objection against the Sein zum Tod."[16] Indeed, in his mind my care for Being was inseparable from my care for my own Being.

Obviously, his own approach to death was not professorial at all; it was the outburst of a deep existential concern for love and intersubjectivity - the kind of approach that was bound to cause in the young students of Kyoto the lasting and overriding impression to which he refers in the last book that he dictated.[17]

2 - Presence and Immortality.

Marcel's many elaborations on the will and on faith in the Metaphysical Journal do indeed shed light on his repeated references to love as the foundation of his faith in immortality. In his lecture, "Presence et immortalite," which was delivered in Rabat, Sao Paolo, and other South American cities in 1951 and was thereafter published as a chapter in his book by the same name, he makes his case in two steps.

First he shows that immortality is possible, and then he goes on to establish its necessity and by the same token its factual actuality. He starts with the simple observation that sometimes we may be conversing for hours with someone who is "perceptibly" in the same room with us and yet not feel his presence. We may even come to realize that he is rather "infinitely far more distant from us than a certain beloved one who is presently miles away from us or even does no longer belong to our world."[18]

Let us leave out for the time being the last clause. The fact that between the one who is in the room and myself there is "sense-transmitted communication" but no "communion" raises the following vital question: what then is presence, the kind of presence that my friend makes me feel and which does also prompt me to be present to him? In order to answer this question, a twofold fact is worth pondering. Indeed, for one thing, sense communication is obviously not enough to generate communion and may even set up between the other and myself such an impenetrable barrier that it will literally force me to become alien evento myself--because, as Marcel comments in connection with the above mentioned hypothesis: "the other comes between me and myself thereby making me somehow incomprehensible to myself, as though I were a perfect stranger, and as a result he finally makes it impossible for meeven to adhere to my own words"--;[19] whereas on the other hand the spatio-temporal distance is sometimes no obstackle to that refreshing and wonderful spiritual presence that we are trying to understand. Such a realization should lead us to wonder why we should not make room also for a spiritual relation of that kind between ourselves and our dead ones.

Marcel sheds further light on the possibility that is now being examined. Indeed, in the quotation that we just transcribed we heard him saying that at one point the subject of our case may not even be able to make himself "present" to the fellow waiting with him in the room because of his having been paralyzed to the point of no longer being in a position even to"adhere tohis own words"...This links Marcel's remarks on presence to another argument that he makes in Searchings which we will preface here with the following reasoning.

What he just observed is tantamount to saying that "our spiritual works" cannot be "effective" if the spirit is not "present" in them. We are entitled therefore to conclude that, vice versa, if a page written by a great philosopher can change the world during his lifetime, it is not the ink and the shape of the letters printed in the paper that are to be credited for it; it is rather to the life of his spirit which manifests itself through them that we have to trace such a wonder. The ink and the letters alone cannot make that miracle, as is clear from the fact that if a child were to write some words hundreds of times in compliance with a certain punishment and therefore without putting his soul in them, the material page that he would hand to the teacher would never be able to change the world. At this point we are in a position to face a case parallel to the one just described by Marcel.

Indeed, just as in the aforementioned hypothesis the fact that Marcel felt entitled to visualize a post mortem type of presence on the grounds that even among the living there are non-spatial cases of spiritual communion, why then should we not be allowed to stretch our own remarks concerning the non-spatial spiritual influence of both a philosopher through his printed thoughts and a musician through his published scores by extrapolating the impact that the thoughts of those spirits make from a distance during their life-times to the lasting bearing that they do in fact have on future generations even after their own demise, as history's records bear out? The proposed extrapolation is warranted on the grounds that the only alternative to it would be its blunt negation on the basis of a mere absence of biological processes, which essentially are no more than purely spatio-temporal conditions and had therefore already been transcended to the satisfaction of everyone concerned, as well as on the lack of spatial vicinity between living authors and their distant audiences or readers, which has proven equally harmless throughout the history of music and literature. For what the conductors and the readers are interpreting with such a delight are not dead symbols but living thoughts and feelings insofar as they are still vitally linked to their sources despite the spatial distance that separates the symbols from the authors. Indeed, if those symbols were not the conduit of a fresh and living stream of thought and feelings they would never have a true appeal on our spirits. As it is now, therefore, we are witnessing a warm communication among real spirits, and such a communication is not only totally independent of the biological processes that are simultaneously taking place in the living bodies of the authors--who at that time might even be on the brink of death for that matter--but would also even survive the sudden death of the writer or the musician if the latter occurred during the performance of a work of art or the reading of a philosophical masterpiece. The likelihood of immortality is therefore evident. But, is immortality "necessary"?

As announced before, this was only a preface to an argument which was actually presented by Marcel in Searchings, and was concerned with that necessity. His reflections were prompted by the following objection:

> It could be said that we are dealing
> with purely subjective moods, with
> psychological impulses, that in no
> way change what we would probably
> call reality. But just what is this
> reality people generally like to
> talk about? If it is not outright
> fate, it is at least a controllable
> process by which the body--whether
> of a loved one or anyone else--
> becomes a cadaver and eventually

disintegrates. However, limiting
the reality of death to this
biological process, whether
consciously or not, means
capitulating to the grossest
materialism. That is so obvious I
am almost ashamed to call it to your
attention.

Marcel tries to overcome so crass a materialism by
resorting to a kind of second reflection on a universal
linguistic phenomenon that betrays a deep human conviction. Indeed, the fact that we refer to Moliere,
Rembrandt or Mozart in the "present tense" when we speak
of their works calls for a sufficient reason. Now, such
an account cannot be "their bodies, that have long
decayed," as Marcel puts it, nor their material work
alone, for if Moliere's work, for instance, had been
written in a language that a cataclysm had suddenly
wiped out of the earth and thereby rendered absolutely
unintelligible to the current generations, it would not
at the present time warrant our reference to Moliere as
actually saying "this" or "that" today. If he says
something to us today it is because something is being
conveyed from him to us through that work. Says Marcel:

...what perdures in material form,
and what will continue to perdure,
are spirit and thought. If it is to
have any personal appeal, it will
have to be adequately related to our
spirit and our thinking. History
shows that events can intervene
which actually make a certain

language no longer intelligible.

Yet Marcel may have overlooked another possibility that would account for the survival of the masterpieces themselves as prompters of living interpretations throughout the centuries and would make the survival of their authors unnecessary. Such is the third world proposed by Karl Popper, namely, the world of culture which, once created by the spirit, acquires a total independence and subsists on its own. This serious objection calls for Marcel to establish a need for the creator's continuing intervention without which the work of art would not subsist in its communicative effectiveness. This, though, seems to be impossible. At least the following very serious doubt could be cast on such a need. Let us imagine-- a very likely hypothesis indeed-- that an artist barely had time to bring to this world an incomparable creation which is now in the hands of the art lovers--and even of the interpreters if it is a theater play or a symphony. Immediately thereafter he lost his mind by going into a prolonged coma. The fact that there is no way to trace the current success of his production to any current causal activity on his part seems to belie Marcel's contention altogether. From that point of view, the following inference that he tries may not transcend the level of "wishful thinking": "If the phrase 'out-live'--he says--"is true, from the standpoint of time, then it is true in an infinitely more pround sense that they are the ones who actually outlive us. Here the prefix `out' means about the same as `over' in the phrase `fly over.' Mozart and Moliere outlive us and illuminate us from above."[20] Indeed, to say the least, it is hard to say why it should be so...

But Marcel seems to be on a better ground when he tries another argument. In "Présence et immortalité" he shows how little importance he attaches to the positivist contention that an alleged co-presence with someone who by now has already been reduced to a bundle of bones and a handful of ashes must by force be the result of a purely subjective feeling. He resorts to the scientific level, where he finds facts which he hopes will impress his adversary. "But if experience is consulted without a bias," he writes, "it will dismiss out of hand rash and inadequate remarks of that sort. For a fact so rigorously established as is telepathy suffices to convince us that there are ways of co-presence which cannot be reduced to the type of juxtaposition implied by our daily sort of communication with other men. Those who have conducted the most serious research on telepathy—and I have in mind, for instance, not only Garrington but also Price—have been forced to acknowledge that such phenomena presuppose a specific type of unity among beings."[21]

However, Marcel would not claim that such a scientific verification proves indeed the presence of the dead ones. He certainly grants that it proves the possibility of a certain survival. "In the first place"—he writes again in Présence et immortalité—"I do not think that those researches are unimportant as far as the problem of the mere survival is concerned. A certain number of clear-cut facts are difficult to account for if we do not resort to the hypothesis of an entelechy that survives what we call death. Such an hypothesis is indeed the simplest and most economical one and it may even prompt the hope that through it we might reach a kind of rudimentary verification."[22] But what he has in mind in the beloved one's death is a far cry from a mere survival. As he puts it himself: "mourning...[where] it is kept alive from within by love,...seems to be accompanied by the protestation in the second person: `You cannot simply have disappeared; if I believed that I would be a traitor."[23] Furthermore, leaving out the hypothetical method of science, he adds: "the presence as I evoked it is supra-hypothetical. It gives rise to an assurance which is invincible and inseparable from the kind of love that transforms the lover into an oblation, and it comes through outbursts such as this: `I am sure that you remain present to me, and such a certainty depends on the fact that you never cease helping me, and that may be you are of a greater help to me now than you were when you were on earth."[24] It is clear that the characteristics of presence are totally different from those of survival. But among their differences the following one stands out, namely, that whereas presence is decisively "active," survival is not supposed to be so; and this makes presence so unique that it warrants a thorough examination, not only of the possibility of its essential traits, but also of their factual evidence.

Concerning the possibility of such an ontological presence, the first thing to realize is that the presence of the other cannot be judged by objective criteria because it comes down to a very special presence of Being piercing our world through this or that particular pensée pensante, and we all know that Being's presence can never be objective. It simply manifests itself beyond any doubt, and such imposition is to be accepted, or else the possibility of self-evident knowledge disappears altogether. A quotation to which we referred before says it clearly. "I think in particular of creation," he writes, "and very specially of the dramatical and the musical creations. For example, it is enough to remember the way in which a melodic idea arises: it comes along, it takes over our mind. Where does it come from? Does it come from myself or from somewhere else? Such a distinction, that reflection shows to be meaningless in this connection, presupposes an illusory topography. For it does not make sense to assume that I constitute a limited territory and to wonder whether or not that idea took origin within such a territory."[25] According to Marcel the territory-type of man does not exist, and his mind would not change in that respect even if such a territory were construed as an all-encompassing subconscious mind.

In the second place, if we can be sure that God, the infinite subject, exists, by the same token the possibility of such an ontological presence precisely in the form of a subject will have to be accepted. Hence, the question: Can we be sure of it? Granted that God's existence cannot be proved, that is "objectively" established. But nothing prevents reason from reaching a rational certainty of his actuality. Kant, for one, showed that such a rational maneuver was possible, and he showed it without claiming to know that God exists; and he did not apologize for his absolutely necessary belief in the divine reality, of which he rather bragged.[26] On his part, Michele Federico Sciacca, carrying St. Augustine's argument to the end, showed that either the eternal subsistent Truth that energizes our minds corresponds to Being's actuality in the form of an infinite subject capable of knowing it, or nothing at all makes sense.[27] In particular, the possibility of

the ontological presence of "the other" was given much
thought by Gabriel Marcel. In his Metaphysical Journal,
for instance, he accounted for interpersonal communication through the selves' foundation in the Divine Mind.
Repeating Clarisses's words in Le Quattuor in fa diéze,
he wrote: "God is that in which thoughts communicate,
the real foundation of the communication between individualities."28 Then, in Présence et immortalité, he
became more specific as to the way in which intersubjectivity takes place through love.

In his view, the true love for one another is
possible only if the lovers share in the light of Being.
This amounts to saying that true love is possible only
if the lovers approach one another in their capacity as
participation in Being, and of this indeed they can be
sure only in the light of Being. But when it comes
endowed with those ontological characteristics, love
cannot be conditioned by the limitations of the other or
even by the limitations of the object's essence. Marcel
puts it very clearly as he refers to love among humans:
"love bears on what is beyond essence, love is the act
by which a thought, by thinking a freedom, is made free.
In this sense love extends beyond any possible judgment,
for judgment can only bear on essence--and love is the
very negation of essence (in this sense love extends
beyond any possible judgment, for judgment can only bear
on essence--and love is the very negation of essence (in
this sense it implies faith in the perpetual renewal of
being itself, the belief that nothing ever is, that
nothing ever can be irremediably lost)."29 Viewed from
the other side, this means that not only does the lover
not have to be conditioned by the appearances, either
essential or accidental, of "the other;" it also

entails that the beloved one is guaranteed patience and mercy on the lover's part on the grounds that Being shows infinite resilience in the beloved one even in the midst of his gravest sins. Marcel does not mince his words in this respect: "only for love is the individuality of the beloved immune against disintegration and crumbling away, so to speak, into the dust of abstract elements. But it is only possible to maintain the reality of the beloved because love posits the beloved as transcending all explanation and all reduction. In this sense it is true to say that love only addresses itself to what is eternal, it immobilises the beloved above the world of genesis and vicissitude."[30] This is indeed what is called loving our neighbor "in God." It is true therefore to say "that the love which prohibits all reflection has been subject to divine mediation."[31]

An immediate corollary to this is that if the lover is in fact influenced by the necessity of the so-called evidence of the beloved's disqualification in terms of certain inflexible and cruel moral "codes," we can conclude for sure that he is not actually steering his love toward the real Being of the beloved. There is a passage in Présence et immortalité that supports this position one hundred percent: "We might say that intersubjectivity comes down to the fact of being together in the light. Here again we must proceed negatively in order to approach the positive essence towards which reflection ought to be steered. If in the presence of the other I am saddled with afterthoughts about him, or vice-versa I accuse him of doing the same about me, which amounts to the same thing, it is quite clear that we are not together in the light. I am casting my own shadow on myself, and this results in the impossibility for him to be present to me and for me to be present to him."[32] But by the same token Marcel can establish a safe criterion to decide if the beloved one who passed away is present to the surviving lover. Indeed, I can be sure that I am present to him if I can say with full confidence: "We are together in the light, or rather, whenever I detach myself from myself, whenever I stop casting my own shadow on myself, I have access to a light which is your light, not in the sense that you are its source, but insofar as you beam in it and have it irradiate and reverberate on me."[33] After all, it is always the same premise, the same essential relation between the real demands of my own Being and the reality of my will's object, a relation which is based altogether on the nature of the will. For we heard Marcel defining the will in these terms: "It seems to me that will is in some way to commit oneself: by which I mean to commit or bring into play one's own reality; to throw oneself into what one wills. I would be tempted to go so far as to say that to will is to affirm: `I depend on that (I will only be if that is), hence that depends on me'."[34]

As far as the case of our beloved dead one is concerned, that presence that the surviving lover "wills" through the aforementioned outburst is really necessary to him because he loves it on the grounds that "such a presence is then a revealing one, that is, it makes me be more fully myself than I would be without it."[35] Indeed, there is nothing that my Being needs more than what is necessary, under the circumstances, for its present growth. Thus the presence of the beloved dead one comes through a kind of silent dialogue between him and the living surviving lover, just as the presence of a friend still living on this earth comes through a real verbal dialogue. The latter, says Marcel, is an experience that "One might call at best an existential experience. Because it is not so much the content of the other's words that exert on me such a stimulating action as himself saying them and supporting them with his whole Being."[36] This unmistakable feeling is one that in the unfinished play included in Présence et immortalité Edith, the mourning mistress of her own just deceased brother-in-law, defines so well as the feeling of a lack of "absence." She can therefore describe to the visiting priest in the following terms the difference she sees between her relation to the dead one and the one that still links her to the living husband: "That feeling of absence that a dear one would never be able to arouse in us, I experience it in regard to my husband with an awful intensity..."[37] Edith claims that in her relation with her lover she is only living her faith, and she contends that the same cannot be said of the priest, who in turn seems to fall into contradiction and inconsistency. This is why, when Rev. Seveilhac surmises that nothing in reality matches such a feeling,she vehemently protests: "The bottom-line is that according to you the dead ones are no longer there and in this you do not think differently from those who do not believe. Whatever the glorious but unimaginable existence you grant them may be...to you they are no longer living beings. On the contrary, myself I hold that the true dead ones, those who are truly dead, are only those that we do no longer love."[38] No wonder that even her approach to religion should be different from that of the priest. "In my view, the only religion that counts," she snaps back at the expression of shock shown in Mr. Seveilhac's face, "is one that ushers us into a different world where the miserable barriers that separate the beings of flesh and bones from one another vanish and are replaced by love and charity." And she adds: Yes indeed, I feel him close to me, always closer to me. And I revolt against the idea that such a feeling may be a guilty one. After all, it is life."[39] This, of course, is the same as to say: it is part of the necessary development of humans. Yet, there is still a sense of a risky decision in that position...

Indeed, we established that the "possibility" of experiencing the presence of the other even if he is dead fits perfectly in Gabriel Marcel's philosophy. As for the "factual evidence" of individual cases, even Marcel recognizes that it does to exist in the proper sense of the word. For even if the criteria are assumed to be sound and reliable--and they are indeed--, their application may be subject to more subjective arbitrariness than is desirable, the end result being doubt and hesitation. But, to the extent that this makes room for freedom, is it not all the better for that? Hence, he can say: "Our world is structured in such a way that there are plenty of reasons around me to despair and view death as the annihilation and the miserable key word of the incomprehensible existence into which I have been incomprehensibly thrown. Yet, a deeper reflection may show the same world as being simultaneously thus constituted that I can become conscious of the power that I was left with of refusing those negative appearances and denying to death the above mentioned ultimate reality. There lies the meaning of the word `unverifiable' to which I have resorted."[40] As to those positive clues, he adds, they "have a consistence which is barely sufficient to do their job; if they were real proofs, they would annul and void my freedom in the face of death. As a result, just as it happens to certain naive minds, both life and death would be stripped of their seriousness for me, and in my view sacrifice would lose its tragical and ultimate value."41

Once on this track, Marcel could not put an end to his treatment of death without agreeing with Peter Wust's theme on "the metaphysical worth of the risk in its capacity as the condition of possibility of human existence taken in accordance with its mysterious specificity."42 But we should not forget that in his mind--as shown in section 3 of chapter IV--, the love of God is linked so tightly to our perfectibility, that the ensuing demand of immortality expressed through an act of will within the modality of necessity cannot help but being endowed with metaphysical certainty, and thus add weight to the positive side of the risky decision.

Claude Mauriac zeroed in on a quotation that gives us the whole of Marcel's philosophy of death. Concerning the possibility of an absolute and irreversible destruction of his own Being, he once exploded in the following words: "If indeed I agreed to it, it would be for me a frightful collapse."43

Under the circumstances, who can doubt that immortality was indeed a matter of "will" and, therefore, of indubitability, for Marcel as a straightforward-looking Freedom?

footnotes

[1]TrW, p. 231; see Peccorini, F.L., Gabriel Marcel: La "Razón de Ser" en la "Participación" (Barcelona: Juan Flors, Editor, 1959), p. 254, footnote #119. See Also EchE, pp. 159-160.

[2]Gabriel Marcel interrogé par Pierre Boutang, pp. 10-11. See also TrW, p. 20.

[3]Searchings, p. 59.

[4]O.c., p. 60.

[5]TrW, p. 131.

[6]Gabriel Marcel et la pensée allemande, pp. 35-36.

[7]See TrW, p. 121.

[8]O.c., p. 122.

[9]See O.c., pp. 12-13 and Searchings, p. 61.

[10]TrW, p. 123.

[11]Ibid.

[12]O.c., p. 127.

[13]O.c., p. 124.

[14]CrF, p. 141.

[15]TrW, p. 127.

[16]Entretiens autour de Gabriel Marcel, p. 227.

[17]EChE, p. 281.

[18]PI, p. 187.

[19]O.c., pp. 187-188.

20Searchings, pp. 63-64.

[21]PI, p. 187.

22PI, p. 191.

[23]Searchings, p. 64.

24PI, p. 191.

[25]O.c., p. 190.

[26]See Peccorini, On to the World of Freedom, last chapter.

[27]See Peccorini, From Gentile...pp. 168-171 and 182-183.

[28]MJ, pp. 61-62. See Peccorini, "The Ontological Route in the Light of Marcel and Sciacca," in Giornale di Metafisica, 28 (1973), p. 513.

29MJ, p. 64.

[30]MJ, pp. 62-63.

31MJ, p. 66.

[32]PI, p. 189.

33PI, p. 191.

[34]MJ, pp. 185-186.

35PI, p. 187.

[36]O.c., p. 188.

[37]PI, p. 225.

[38]Ibid.

[39]Ibid.

[40]O.c., p. 192.

[41]Ibid.

[42]Ibid.

[43]Claude Mauriac, "Gabriel Marcel et l'invisible," in Le Figaro, 7/24/76.

Chapter VI

The Nuptial Bond of Life
as an Ethical Arrow for a Lay World

As pointed out in the previous chapter, man's position vis-à-vis his own death and the death of the beloved one winds up being a matter of a freezing choice. But man's freedom is faced with more frightening decisions without which human existence would not even be possible.

1 - The Self in the Isolation of its Freedom.

Marcel holds his freedom to be a datum, furthermore, the most important datum on which his moral life rests altogether. And if he cannot doubt of his own being free it is because he considers himself as the judge without appeal of his own freedom. "It is beyond the power of anyone"--he writes--"to reject the decision by which I assert my freedom, and this assertion is ultimately bound up with the consciousness that I have of myself."[1] On the other hand, to the extent that the whole social life--which is founded in the feeling of responsibility--would crumble without the foundation of freedom, he is glad that freedom is so undeniable. He makes it very clear that he is glad by appropriating Jasper's words: "We are conscious of our freedom when we recognize what others expect from us. It is upon us that the fulfillment or shirking of these obligations depends; we cannot, accordingly, deny with any seriousness that we have thus to make a decision about something, and so about ourselves, and that thus we are responsible. Further, anyone who refused to accept this responsibility would ipso facto make it impossible for himself to exact anything from other men."[2]

It is clear, of course, that according to Marcel freedom unveils itself to us, not through any sense of self-independence nor in the fact of doing what we feel like doing, but through the feeling of our own responsibility. Indeed, to do as one pleases amounts to following one's own desires. Now, according to Marcel, it is problematic--to say the least-- that wish and will match each other. To him it is rather the case that "It might well be--the stoics first saw this, and all the subsequent thinkers who drew their inspiration from stoicism--that will is essentially opposed to desire. Do I not chiefly, if not exclusively, seem to myself to be free only when I succeed in using my will in opposition to my own desire--provided, of course, that it is not just a question of a mere whim, but that the will is embodied in acts which themselves form part of what I call reality? From this point of view one might say that the will appears as a resistance to seductions to which desire exposes me, seductions which, if I yield to them, are quick to turn into compulsions."[3] But, by the same token, his conception of happiness must follow suit. Happiness, in other words, is not achieved by yielding to all our desires. He elaborates on this point as follows: "...it is only too clear that there are countless instances in which I by no means do what I want to do; and we have the support of irrefutable evidence when we say that certain beings in captivity, in conditions, that is, which would involve the reduction to a minimum of what we commonly think of as independence have nevertheless enjoyed a much deeper experience of their inner freedom than they would have been able to do in what we all call normal life."[4]

It is clear, therefore, that according to Marcel the only specifying element of the free act, as counter-distinguished from the act of desire, consists in such an indifference of judgment about the object that winds up showing the latter as a means only, never as an end. In other words, an act done out of fascination for an object would still qualify as a free act if it were simultaneously viewed only as a means to the ultimate end. It would not be free, though, if it were-- abnormally as this may be-- perceived as an end only. By the same token, therefore, Marcel might as well accept the following conclusion that ensues from the same premises, namely, that, whether or not our behavior is good, freedom amounts to the mere control of our love. This, of course, would enable him to agree, not only with St. Thomas, but also with St. Bernard and Malebranche. For, according to the latter, our will is the faculty that leads us to love the Good as such-- and by implication God himself--in an irresistible way; and this does equally entail that it is impossible for any particular good, which as such cannot fully satiate our natural appetite, to engage our love in full. This means that it can merely allure our will in its capacity as means to the supreme good, or at most, as an intermediate end subordinate to our ultimate destiny. Freedom, therefore, would come down to the power bestowed upon our will in virtue of which the latter can zero in its love on this particular means or intermediate end rather than on any other; a power, which is

practically inseparable from both the accompanying
indifference of judgment that was mentioned above and
the creatures' ability to inchoate the full satiety that
we long for.5 But such a power is, in turn, fully
compatible with disorderly choices, that is, with its
own misuse--although the latter is not essential to
Freedom, which lies only in the control of our loving
stream. Indeed, one can visualize a situation in
which, while actually being dragged by the attraction of
one particular good, we still face other objects which
not only are perceived as being equally able to inchoate
our own happiness, but could also be freely pursued by
us, and yet we prefer to insist on the former instead.
In fact, for healthy persons this is the case any time
they are allured by finite goods. Then even if at first
our choice of an object were blind, by deciding not to
give it up for other objects perceived as being also
appealing we clearly manifest a genuine consent to it on
the part of our will. To put it in Malebranche's words,
"Through my consent, that movement, which was before
naturally indeterminate, cannot help but suddenly become
steered towards such a good, and this also happens
according to human nature. Yet, the way in which I
consent to such a movement is rather awkward, to say the
least. For, what do I do thereto? I drag my feet and,
while realizing that I should turn my attention away
from the object, I take my time to do so, thereby
showing that I still enjoy it and am holding on to it."6
This shows freedom as being fully inscribed to the
service of the law of love, as St. Augustine had put it
many centuries ago: "Lex itaque libertatis, lex
charitatis," i.e. the law of freedom is the law of love.
And consequently, the "true" freedom cannot be other
than the freedom which is essentially related to the

"true" love, which is the love of the Supreme Good. Marcel understood it perfectly well. But by the same token, he concluded that if freedom subsists through its own misuse, our will needs a special virtue to steer itself in the right direction and thus be able to make the right choice. And he, for one, could not help but associate such a moral virtue with an intellectual virtue that rids the subject of the one-sidedness of fanaticism and thereby does give him also the necessary serenity not to overreact with hatred against the moral blindness of the fanatic person. Such an intellectual virtue--which presupposes the moral disposition to fairness-- comes down to a special penetration into the sense of finiteness which translates itself in turn into a real mastery of the indifference of judgment. As a result, such a serenity of judgment enables the virtuous person to keep his ears open to all possible suggestions concerning the course of action that is likely to pro- mote love and contribute to the perfection of all the participants in the human dialogue. There is a passage in Marcel's Mystery of Being which sums up this whole important point:

> One might add that this assurance of
> being myself can be dimmed, as a
> light can be dimmed, when I undergo
> a process of alienation of which (we
> may note parenthetically) Marxism
> has diagnosed only one particular
> modality. In particular it is clear
> that there is alienation so soon as
> there is obsession or a fixed idea.
> This implies that the state of
> interior dialogue is reduced and

diminished, to give way to a unity of a lower order; and that is what we always see in fanatics. But we must note, from another angle, that the preservation of the interior dialogue is always bound up with the act of keeping oneself open to the other, that is to say with being ready to welcome whatever positive contribution the other can make to me, even if this contribution is liable to modify my own position. We must admit, however, that we can be open to others in this way only on certain conditions. When I am faced by a fanatic, it is impossible for me not to feel on the defensive. This is necessarily so because the fanatic, inasmuch as he is a fanatic, ceases to be an interlocutor, and becomes only an adversary who handles what he calls his ideas as offensive weapons. The result is that I am forced to find some defensive armour for myself, and as what is properly called discussion is shown to be impossible, I feel bound in the end either to meet violence with violence, or to refuse the battle. I need hardly add that the most serious fault is that of forcing on its opponents the cruel compulsion of falling themselves into the same fault. The Saint alone, it would seem, can escape this compulsion, but only, we may add, provided that he possesses, on the contrary, the highest degree of that virtue of strength which at present seems to be ill understood by a vast number of Christians.[7]

If, however, we reduce the essence of freedom to such a power of controlling our love, and recognize that the right use of such a power rests on an intellectual precondition, namely, the self's control on our outlook on finite reality for which we feel equally responsible, it is impossible to keep on claiming that it is the will itself that is free. We must rather state that it is only the self that is free, and that he would be free, and therefore responsible, even if, while being victimized by a seizure of fanaticism, he were to fail to act fairly. After all, he would still be responsible for not having duly controlled his outlook on finite reality. Of course, Marcel's firm conviction about this personal characteristic of human freedom makes him reluctant readily to accept excuses based on a presumed lack of freedom. He acknowledges that quite often he is all too quick to excuse himself in his own eyes for what he did, but then, he adds, "there is something in me which refuses to countenance this way of proving my innocence. The symptom of this refusal"-- he goes on to say--" is a feeling of uneasiness, as though I had to admit that I have no right to locate in something external (let us say in the circumstances themselves) the responsibility for what was in spite of everything my own act."[8] Indeed, acting without such a right woulɑ amount to giving up the duty of steering the uniform growth of my own Being by allowing my whims to enslave me for ever. "If I protest," he writes, "it is because I have a vague feeling that I cannot win such an acquittal except at the expense of my own being." To say it bluntly, "if I allow to my desires, which are in some way detached from me, the power to reduce me to slavery, I put myself more and more at their mercy; almost as a man who has once yielded to the demands of a blackmailer finds that he is caught up in a web from which there is no escape."9

No doubt that Marcel's insistence on my own responsibility is founded in a deep metaphysical assumption, namely, that I am not my life, but the one who is called upon to control it. He elaborates on this in one of the milestones of his production. In Être et Avoir, keeping in mind his life insofar as it is his own way of sharing in the common life of men, he writes:

> But it is an indisputable fact that
> my life, understood in this sense--
> i.e. as participation in this common
> world--may become for me an object
> of judgment, approval or
> condemnation. My life is something
> I can evaluate. An essential datum.
> But what am I, this I which
> evaluates it? Impossible to cling
> to the fiction of a transcendental
> I. The I that evaluates is the same
> as the I that is judged. It must be
> added that my life, just in so far
> as I lead it, is, as it were, shot

through by an implicit evaluation
(whether adhered to or disobeyed;
for I may be leading a life which
something within me is continually
protesting against with a dull
insistence).[10]

And, what is still more important in regard to the lay
approach to Ethics that we are trying to establish in
this chapter, such an evaluation proceeds according to
the best possible criterion, namely human nature insofar
as the latter tells us not what we are, but what we
ought to be. The distinction is indispensable. If we
take human nature in the former sense, the implication
is that man is one more thing, and that he can be known
objectively as things are. The "ought" implication, on
the other hand, comes down to an acknowledgement that
man is what he freely becomes. Again, the objective
approach makes communication altogether impossible, for,
as Marcel puts it, "if we cling to a mode of objective
definition, it will always be in our power to say that
the Thou is an illusion." Fortunately, such an approach
is not the only alternative, for Marcel calls our attention to the fact that "the term essence is itself
extremely ambiguous; by essence we can understand either
a nature or a freedom. It is perhaps of my essence qua
freedom to be able to conform myself or not to my
essence qua nature. It may be of my essence to be able
not to be what I am; in plain words, to be able to
betray myself. Essence qua nature is not what I reach
in the Thou. In fact if I treat the Thou as a He, I
reduce the other to being only nature; an animated
object which works in some ways and not in others. If,
on the contrary, I treat him and apprehend him qua

freedom, I apprehend him qua freedom because he is also freedom, and is not only nature."[11]

It is therefore such a core of my Being, such a peak of my personality--the one that remains unchanged throughout the ups and downs of my unstable life and thus constitutes the true "ontological permanent"--that is really free and can as such face its life to the point of being able to judge it.

2 - Respect for Humanity and the Creature's Humility.

Implicit in this guiding power that human essence qua freedom wields lies a tension towards the dynamic perfection that gives meaning to our freedom. "It may be said..."-writes Marcel--"that no concrete philosophy is possible without a constantly renewed yet creative tension between the I and those depths of our being in and by which we are."[12] In other words, it is because our "essence-freedom" entices the dynamism of our will and thereby constitutes the ontological law of the latter that our becoming, which is our way of being, can be prompted. But this is enough to place Marcel and Sartre poles apart from one another. For indeed it brings to light the awesome chasm that separates the philosophy of humility of the former from the philosophy of the absolute moral autonomy, from which the ethical existentialism of the latter takes its inspiration. No wonder Marcel had to write the following in his criticism of Sartre's Nausée: "Can it be legitimate to say that, for the human being, being is equivalent to doing? Is this not something more than a simplification?" And he answered his question positively as he had to do since he had already drawn a gap between his own Being and his life: "Is it not a misapprehension of what is deepest and most significant in the nature of man? How can it be right to ignore the distinction, commonly made, between what a man is and what he does? Does not this statement alone reveal the inadequacy of Sartre's ontology?"[13] It is obvious that Marcel, for whom ontology is based on the ontological depths of the "pensee pensante," is blaming Sartre in the strong concluding statement of the foregoing passage precisely for disregarding completely the profound respect that "humanity," in its capacity as the "essence-freedom", deserves. Furthermore, since within his conception, insofar as it is based on an essential respect for humanity, man and humility are inseparable, his goal can only be to divert our attention from Sartre's shortcomings to Kant's deep ethical approach by updating the latter. "Our aim"--he says--"is to allow ourselves a more precise view of the nature of the venerable (le reverentiel) which must be posited if humility is to be true and significant. Here again it is important to refer to Kant; it would not be easy nowadays to agree with the view of respect which he gave in his Critique of Practical Reason, but that by no means implies that his view is mistaken."[14]

The link between humility and human perfection is therefore worth emphasizing. Another contemporary philosopher, who depended also--at least partially-- on the insights brought forth by Maurice Blondel, gives us the metaphysical reason for it in a concise way. Indeed, while referring to the finiteness of our essence, Michele Federico Sciacca writes: "...far from being considered as changing us...the limit is rather viewed

as that without which we would not be able to be at all.
To say that I am the prisoner of my own Being amounts to
saying that in order to be free I would have not to be
or to be something else."[15] Sciacca insists that our
essential limitation is no suffocating straightjacket;
far from that, he says, it is the only way to be, that
is, to be oneself. To put it in Sciacca's words:
"...the act of setting limits does not take away anything that is necessary or owed by nature to the finite
being itself: it only withholds from it what does not
belong to it and, if given, would make of it a different
being."[16] Furthermore, precisely because being limited
means being created, and because in the case of "free-
doms" being created amounts to being able to control the
stream of love of the will precisely because the will of
men consists in a direct participation in God's will,
then man will be able to get it through prayer from the
One who not only gave him his participatory limitation
but also his shared power. In that sense Sciacca could
write that created freedom "does not found itself, but
founds all other acts through the act by means of which
it recognizes itself as having been founded."[17] This
makes prayer an essential element of human freedom's
foundation insofar as, to use Xavier Zubiri's words.
"Without religation and without the religating one man's
freedom would be man's greatest weakness and his most
radical source of despair. With religation and with
God, on the other hand, his liberty constitutes his
greatest power, which is so great, that it makes up his
own person, his own Being, a Being which is in him while
facing everything else, including his own life...Hence
man is not his own existence, it is rather the latter
that is his."[18]

What better setting could we find for the Marcellian mystical outburst which comes at the summit of his elaboration on creative fidelity, which, in turn, constitutes the zenith of freedom? In it the appeal to God emerges from my own Being because the latter is shown to be essentially religated to God and God, in turn, appears as being built into my own Being. Although we quoted it already in a different context, that passage warrants a full citation again because it represents the quintessence of Marcel's philosophy:

> Hence this ground of fidelity which necessarily seems precarious to us as soon as we commit ourselves to another who is unknown seems on the other hand unshakable when it is based not, to be sure, on a distinct apprehension of God as someone other, but on a certain appeal delivered from the depths of my own insufficiency ad summam altitudinem;

The essential source of this appeal is clearly located in the depths of my own essence; and it enables Marcel to root humility also in the very core of our own Being. He goes on to add:

> I have sometimes called this the absolute resort. This appeal presupposes a radical humility in the subject; a humility which is polarized by the very transcendence of the one it invokes. Here we are, as it were, at the juncture of the

most stringent commitment and the
most desperate expectation. It
cannot be a matter of counting on
oneself, on one's own resources, to
cope with this unbounded commitment;
but in the act in which I commit
myself, I at the same time extend an
infinite credit to Him to whom I did
so; Hope means nothing more that
this.[19]

This conception shows also that to love oneself "truly"
is to love oneself "in humility," and that an atheistic
attitude is essentially proud and challenging. "As to
self-love," he tells us, "it is easy to discern the
complete opposition which exists between an idolatrous
love and a charity towards oneself which, far from
treating the self as a plenary reality sufficing to
itself, considers it as a seed which must be cultivated,
as a ground which must be readied for the spiritual or
even for the divine in this world. To love oneself in
this second sense is not the same as self-complacency,
but is rather an attitude towards the self which permits
its maximum development."[20] It is, in other words, to
love oneself with the fullness of the will's love
because the will, by striving to love Being in full,
i.e. by striving for the fullness of its own love,
brings the person up to the peak of its own perfection.
In turn, this identity between the love of Being and the
love of the self shows that any conception of the self
that is not based on the "pensee pensante" but on absolute self-sufficiency and irreceptivity is doomed to
wind up in atheism and idolatrous pride.

Obviously, Marcel could not feel comfortable with it. "What it comes down to"--he writes--"is this (and it is an attitude which seems to me to lay bare the roots of metaphysical pride): for Sartre, to receive is incompatible with being free; indeed, a being who is free is bound to deny to himself that he has received anything. But I wonder if here the author of La Nausee does not fall into one of the worst errors which can be attributed to Idealism."21 Mistaken or not, what is certain is that Sartre had no other outcome available. For, as Marcel puts it, "As soon as receptivity in a spiritual, or even in a living, being is confused with suffering in a material sense (in the sense in which wax suffers the imprint of a seal) it becomes impossible to conceive the concrete and organized relationship between the individual and the world. There remain only two terms of reference: an actuality which is, so to speak, inert, and a freedom which denies it only to assume it in an incomprehensible way at a later stage."22 The allusion to the antithesis "in-itself," "for-itself" is clear in Marcel's passage. But by the same token, we are asked to consider a far more important aspect of Sartre's philosophy.

Once Sartre had denied the constitutive presence of Being in the self, he had no other way but to dig a gap between the in-itself and the for-itself --that is, in Sartre's unconventional view (which openly parts company with the traditional view that had always attributed to Being, one way or the other, a "humanizing" power in man's essence), between the "non-human," Being, and the "human," consciousness--, but by the same token he was bound to leave the self fully unaccounted for. And indeed, he chose to dig such a chasm, as we have it on his own authority. For it is a fact that he openly opposed what we might call "objective interiority," which consists in accounting for subjectivity by means of the objective and challenging presence of Being to the subject. This covers, as an umbrella, not only Sciacca's "ontological synthesis," Marcel's "pensée pensante," and St. Augustine's "eternal truth," but even Heidegger's Dasein; and he was adamant against it to the risk of leaving his own "pure consciousness" unexplained for ever because in his effort to make human freedom as absolute as Descartes had made God's, he had to declare without any objective foundation that the former is the antithesis of what he had already apprehended as the massive and unintelligible "in-itself," which he described as being de trop. In this sense, to him Being does automatically fall to the despicable rank of an "inhuman" element. He writes:

> How can one justify praxis...if one sees in it merely the inessential moment of a radically inhuman process? How can one show it to be a real and material totalization if, through it, what is totalized is Being pure and simple? Man would then become what Walter Biemel, in commenting on Heidegger's works, calls the `bearer of the Opening of Being.'

Indeed, he cannot hide his intention of scoffing at such a conception that he evidently considers erroneous, to say the least. Still writing in the same mood, he goes on to emphasize what he considers Heidegger's philosophical sin:

> This identification is not inapt: if
> Heidegger has praised Marxism, it is
> because he sees in this philosophy a
> way of showing, as Waelhens says of
> Heideggerians, existentialism, `that
> Being is Otherness in me...(and
> that) man...is himself only through
> Being, which he himself is not.'

It is worth considering that according to Michele
Federico Sciacca, it is precisely the fact that Being,
as the transcendental object, is the Other, that constitutes man into an "interior objectivity;" and that in
Kant's view, it is precisely the same fact that makes
transcendental apperception fully "objective" and therefore fit to serve as the foundation of man's total
knowledge. To put it bluntly, Sartre's scorn for such a
fact must necessarily sound strange to anyone who is
familiar with the history of philosophy...And yet,
Sartre is not ashamed of being the only one, perhaps,
who has ever dissociated Being from the constitution of
human knowledge. He rather brags of being the only
philosopher who is right in that respect...He goes on
scorning Heidegger's position:

> But every philosophy that
> subordinates the human to the
> nonhuman--be it an existentialist or
> a Marxist idealism--has hatred of
> man as its basis and its
> consequence; History has proved it
> in both cases. One must choose: Man

is from the first himself or he is
from the first other than himself.
And if one chooses the second
doctrine one is nothing but a victim
and an accomplice of real
alienation.[23]

Such was Sartre's final and "unappealable" position that
was solemnly stated in his last major work, La Critique
de la raison dialectique.

At this point we are facing a clear balance. Not
only do we know that Marcel's freedom is a pursuit of an
ontologically detailed plan as opposed to Sartre's
arbitrary unleashing of the for-itself; we do also know
by now why the two French existentialists find themselves at the extreme poles of this antithesis.
Furthermore, after Marcel's elaborations on the why and
the nature of the "pensée pensante" it would be easy to
show that Sartre's misgivings about the "non-human"
character of Being are on a rather weak ground. The
lack of time forces us to leave that task to the reader.
What really counts is that both approaches affect our
ethical conception in totally different ways. Whereas
Marcel's freedom is entirely to the service of human
perfection, Sartre's is absolutely immune to any guiding
values of any kind. Marcel's concept, which makes room
for immoral free acts insofar as they too are the result
of our will's control of its own stream of love, allows
also and mainly for an objective qualitative range of
free acts. The criterion for the latter rests on
freedom's essential subordination to perfection. "No
doubt"--says Marcel--"one might say that what distin-
guishes the free act is that it helps to make me what I

am, as a sculptor might carve me, whereas the contingent or insignificant act, the act which might just as well be performed by anybody, has no contribution to make to this sort of creation of myself by myself."[24] More accurately, the criterion in question comes down to the degree in which that act is significant in regard to the real stake, which is human perfection. This accounts for the fact that although the essence of freedom as a power to control our love can be safeguarded in evil acts and, a fortiori, in merely indifferent acts, it is only the acts that contribute to human improvement that deserve the consideration of the moralist. In the chain of free acts, therefore, the so-called acts of free choice rank among the lowest ones. Only the acts whose stake is a matter of saving or losing our Being should be called really free. Marcel says it most forcefully: "We must...assert most emphatically on the one hand that the `liberté d' indifference' implies that the stake is indifferent, and on the other hand that we can speak of freedom only when the position is reversed and we can see that the stake has a real importance."[25]

Undoubtedly, on the one hand Marcel recognizes that it behooves the free act to be built within the stream of our will, but on the other hand, to him only those acts through which I either create myself or betray my own Being are most genuinely relevant from the point of view of freedom. But this steers the true freedom towards an order of salvation which is both objective and unavoidable. It is unavoidable because it looms at first in the midst of exigencies made by the core of our human nature.

The author of Et_re e_t Av_oi_r alluded to those demands precisely when he wrote: "It is perhaps of my essence qu_a freedom to be able to conform myself o_r no_t to my essence qu_a nature."[26]

3 - Ethical Essentialism and Human Values.

If we can conform ourselves to our essence qu_a nature precisely through our essence qu_a freedom, it follows that the order of values works only through the individual's conscience, which in turn cannot disregard the individual's circumstances. It is, therefore, an order which is both objective and concrete, and this means that it is not a merely ideal or abstract order. In other words, Marcel is not concerned with vague, abstract generalizations about morality; he is bent upon improving the quality of the individual's moral behavior. He works from the level of salvation. This is the reason why he disregarded the advice given to him by his friends at the Sorbonne when the latter, at the end of 1943, urged him not to mind Sartre's childish bluffs because they were aimed altogether and only at gaining publicity points. His concern for the negative and nihilating impact that Satre's La Nausée might cause on the young minds led him to reply as follows: "I was told that I worried too much, that 'these people' liked nothing so much as a scandal, and that, by taking them too seriously, I was playing into their hands. But I believed then, as I do now, that Sartre's philosophy was much too impressive particularly to young people, not to be examined with the utmost seriousness and objectivity."[27] At the end of his promised analysis he concluded with the following words, which show an indubitable moral objectivism: "Sartre has announced that the third volume of his Les Chemins de la Liberté is to be devoted to the praise of the heroes of Resistance. Now I ask you in the name of what principle, having first denied the existence of values or at least of their objective basis, can he establish any appreciable difference between those utterly misguided but undoubtedly courageous men who joined voluntarily the Anti-Bolshevik Legion, on the one hand, and the heroes of the Resistance movement, on the other? I can see no way of establishing this difference without admitting that causes have their intrinsic value and, consequently, that values are real. I have no doubt that Sartre's ingenuity will find a way out of this dilemma; in fact, he quite often uses the words `good' and `bad,' but what can these words possibly mean in the context of his philosophy?"28

It is well known that the "esprit de sérieux" is one of Sartre's most important targets. In this sense, the refutation to which Marcel subjects Sartre's attacks on the same is as good a proof of our author's moral concrete objectivism as the foregoing remarks. As is plain to anyone, according to Sartre the esprit de sérieux fails on two grounds: on the one hand it prevaricates against the Sartrian principle concerning the absolute independence of human subjectivity by treating moral values as data that fully transcend the latter, whereas on the other, it transfers to things' material constitution the property that things have from their ontological structure of being desirable. For instance, says Sartre, if bread is desirable according to such a spirit it is because on the one hand, there is, inscribed in the intelligible world, a value that could be formulated thus: "we must live," whereas, on the other, bread's nutritional character matches such an imperative. Obviously, thus doing away with the so called esprit de serieux necessarily leads to an absolute moral anarchy since, as Marcel points out, in such a case "it is impossible to decide on which principles could rest any hierarchy of values or the modes of expression of our freedom. Evidently, any attempt at introducing such a hierarchy would throw us back into the esprit de serieux."[29]

Marcel, on his part, analyzes in detail the moral consequences that would ensue from the death of God that was prophesied by Nietzsche. Indeed, his findings are not encouraging at all. In his view, once God has been dislodged from human consciences, human values will be doomed to crumble since they are one with the supersensible order, which is organized around an ineffable presence. For, as he sees it, without an absolute Good, "good will appear inseparable from an existential decision which takes place under very determinate circumstances."[30] We will therefore wind up in a pure moral atomism. Under such circumstances there is only one step to this conclusion that has been reached by many a philosopher: Far from the values being endowed with an independent reality, they are a pure creation of the I--and of the empirical I at that, since nowadays it is impossible to have recourse to the transcendental ego, which we gave up in one package with idealism. In fact, under such circumstances, the existentialist philosophies of the present do "rather run the risk of flowing into anarchy, or else, if they want to avoid getting lost in the latter, they will have to make the most dangerous deals with some post-Hegelian doctrines, and most of all, with Marxism."[31]

This amounts to the following most encompassing dilemma. Once God is gone, we are faced with either moral atomism--which is incompatible with the demands of universality that are implied by the ideas of good and justice, and which does also generate a state of endless war, in which the strongest one makes his own ethical criterion prevail until the vanquished one, pushed by his resentment, succeeds in revindicating his own--, or else with a socialist ethics, which hides insurmountable difficulties behind its superficial appeal. Indeed, says Marcel, history "teaches that the individual con- science, in its capacity as bearer of universal values, can rise against the collectivity and oppose a justice believed to be true to the deceptive one that society claims to impose."[32] Now, how could sociology account for such a fact in a logical and consistent vein except by identifying the individual morality in question-- whether the one of Socrates or the one of Christ--as the morality of the forthcoming society and dubbing its bearers as mere precursors of the same? But then a question bounces in front of us: why should the forth- coming morality prevail over the current one? Evidently, its mere chronological place does not warrant such a privilege. Consequently, as Marcel goes on to point out, "it is impossible to get rid of such an inextric- able situation unless we declare that the individual prophet brings a message which involves a transcendent truth."[33] On the other hand, "the only way to dodge the need to introduce the dimension that the word `transcen- dent' expresses fairly well would be to establish as a principle that evolution, in itself, is already a progress."[34] However, history--which offers so many cases of manifest regress during the course of civilization-- does not warrant such a procedure and that principle would necessarily stumble upon the following unremovable difficulty: "In order to locate with precision the point where progress really takes place"--says Marcel--"it will be unavoidably necessary to thresh the events as they succeed one another. But this is impossible unless we resort to one or several criteria equally transcendent in the defined sense."35 Hence, he concludes, "there seems to be no middle alternative: either we abandon all kind of evaluation and lock ourselves into pure subjectivism, or else we keep open the option of a value judgment, but then we automatically bring in the other dimension."36 Under the circumstances, Marcel feels entitled to rely on the system of values, with which everything falls in place. "We might say" --he observes-- "that the value serves as an horizon in which the project or action stands out; or we might add that it functions also as the schematic interpretation that the individual conscience gives itself of the enterprise to which it commits its will when it hurls itself upon any action."37

4 - A Philosophical Ethics for all Seasons : Human Nature As The Criterion of Morals.

Marcel's concrete objectivism and its natural foundation in our "essence qua nature" in combination with our "essence qua freedom" had to lead him to sacrifice the mystical tendency of his whole philosophy towards the Divine Paternity in behalf of the post-Nietzschean world in which we live. He was well aware

indeed that the "death of God" had given rise to the
"agony of man" and that as a result any attempt at
giving birth in the human hearts to the divine union, as
Barth's theology had so effectively done, was meant to
meet with success. Yet, given the massive discomfort of
humanity as a whole, such a decision was bound to lead
to an insoluble problem on which, in Homo Viator, he
invites us to reflect. "Is it fair"-- he askes-- "even
within a perspective which is strictly Christian to
sacrifice in any way whatever our natural Ethics? To
put it briefly, such a sacrifice would come down to the
sanction of a division de facto that tends to grow
between some people, on the one hand, who try to build
up their existence on mystical grounds, and, on the
other hand, those who barely try to survive the incomprehensible, nay, frightening adventure into which they
are conscious of having been thrown by chance, or in
which they find themselves due to the interplay of
inhumane and uncontrollable forces."38

Such an emphasis, though, does not warrant a
complete disregard for the abstract or metaphysical
essences. Marcel,for one, makes human essence the
object of very special affirmations which even sound
somehow Platonic. Thus, for example, in his work titled
Situation perilleuse des valeurs éthiques he complains
that man's essence is in danger: "What is really in a
deadly situation nowadays"--he confides--"is man himself
as a unit, whether we consider him as a concrete whole
or if we focus upon the human species as an unfolding
essence."39 Furthermore, in Le Mystère Familial, upon
referring to "incarnation" in the latter's capacity as
the real breakwater of his philosophy against which all
the assaults from the Idealists crash, he describes it

as "the infinitely mysterious act whereby an essence is
embodied, an act on which Plato had already focused his
meditation and from which modern philosophers divert
their attention solely if, and to the extent that, they
have lost the essential grace of intelligence, which is
wonder."40 As to the objection that most often is
raised against Existentialism, Marcel himself rushes to
make it void. "It should be noted that the philosophies
of existence to which I have been alluding do not necessarily state the priority of existence over the essence.
That is rather an affirmation for which Jean-Paul Sartre
is perhaps nowadays the only one who assumes responsibility. What the above mentioned philosophies bring to
the fare is the impossibility of being satisfied at
present with the traditional conception of the relation
essence/existence according to which the latter falls,
so to speak, in an unintelligible way upon an essence
which was already self-sufficient and on its own."41 If
we keep in mind that according to Marcel to exist is
tantamount to living and that there is a distinction
between the "essence-nature" and the "essence-
freedom,"42 we won't have any reason to disagree with
the foregoing statement. The latter, in turn, entails
that if we really want to have a true knowledge of a
man's Being we cannot rely only on our knowledge of
man's "essence-nature;" a deep penetration into the
man's personality--into his Being insofar as it makes
him a true image of God--becomes necessary. However,
such a penetration cannot take place without love.
"Obviously"--says Marcel--"if I approach the other as a
kind of mechanism which is situated outside of myself
and whose inner spring and way of functioning intrigues
me, even if I succeed in dismantling it for observation's purpose, I will get of him only a superficial

knowledge which is rather a negation of his own real Being. Furthermore"--he goes on to add--"that is indeed a sacreligious and destructive way of knowing, which does entirely deprive its object of its own unique value, thereby degrading it effectively. It is most worth mentioning that such an approach shows that the knowledge of a particular person is inseparable from the love of charity by means of which that being is affirmed as to what constitutes it as a unique creature, or, if you wish, as an image of God."[43] To sum up, by only resorting to the metaphysical essence it is impossible really to know what any concrete man "is" in fact. At most we would be able to deduce therefrom what he "ought to" be. But even if this were possible without considering the circumstances, which according to man's conscience are bound sometimes to mollify the demands of the essence, how could we know what in fact ever happened to that "project" since between the "ought" and the "being" freedom must serve as the necessary link? Marcel, guided by his strong common sense, and referring to a particular behavior, put it in this way: "But those words, `rational animal,' shed no light at all on that particular existence. At most we might mention in this connection the currently accepted notion of project and say that it is part of the human being's project to behave as a rational animal. But such a notion, is it not rather equivocal? At first glance it looks like a psychological truth, but reflection tends to dissipate that appearance, since, from a psychological point of view, it is false to state that every human being has indeed the project of behaving as a rational animal."[44]

Yet, when it comes down to the study of ethics, the "ought" is not any less important than the "is," and

Marcel took it into consideration. For his writings
show very clearly that all his value judgments are
founded in an invariable premise which is the rational
nature taken in all its specifically human respects.
For one thing, according to Marcel it is indubitable
that morality is based on a certain "order," and that
such an order is precisely a "natural" order. In one
word, it is the order of natural virtues. This is the
reason why he could not stand Sartre's scoffing virtue
at large on the grounds that all virtue is a bourgeois
creation. Referring to pp. 109-110 of La Nausée, he
wrote: "Nowhere more than in these pages does Sartre
reveal his resentment against all that is implied by
`social order' and perhaps also by order as such. For
clearly what is being ridiculed is quite different from
mere pharisaism (if it were only that, we would have no
difficulty in agreeing with Sartre); or to be more
exact, all middle-class virtue is regarded as pharisai-
cal, and indeed it may be asked since the publication of
Le Mur and Les Chemins de la Liberté if all virtue
(e.g., conjugal, filial, etc.), with the possible exception of courage, is not treated as middle-class and
consequently as déclassée and valueless."45 Furthermore, it is the order on which the autocreation of our
own Being depends that concerns Marcel; an order that it
is difficult to ascertain whether we invent from scratch
or simply discover it, but an order, after all, that
imposes itself upon us with all the characteristics of a
genuine exigency. In Moi et Autrui he confesses: "How
could we not recognize that the human person cannot be
conceived of independently of the act by means of which
it creates herself, but also that at the same time such
a creation hangs up from a certain order that transcends
it altogether and that the person does not know for sure

if it is her own creation or only her discovery."46
Finally, what is still more important according to
Marcel, such an order is a moral order which is specifically human--and thus essentially different from any
animal, i.e. strictly infra-human, order--and universal.
He even sees the timely and exceptional importance of
that order in connection with certain social phenomena
that our time avails us more and more with, such as the
collective fanatic behavior of the masses when the
latter, acting under a real fascination, fling
themselves blindly to carry out the most incendiary
commands. He puts it most forcefully: "How could we, on
the count that it is prompted by a sort of inebriation,
overlook the fact that such a kind of collective heroism
comes alarmingly close to some infra-humane ways of
behavior and does, as the latter, fall beneath the order
in which the authentic values find their expression?"47
Evidently, in that irrational conduct he misses mostly
the consistency that ensues from the universality of
moral values, mainly from the values of truth and
justice. But precisely because justice is herein associated with universality, he is afraid that his concern
may be misconstrued and finally identified with the type
of inflexible legalism introduced by the naturalists of
the XVIIIth century in which justice was vindicated, as
Descartes had suggested before, more geometrico: with
the least regard for the ups and downs of history--
which lead the human conscience to undergo at times
opposite successive obligations towards itself and the
others. Such a rationalist attitude manifests itself
nowadays through a fetishistic respect for both professional "codes" and, what is still worse, codes of human
rights à la Locke, which are used as logical major
premises to demonstrate that certain actions, which at

face value do not conform to their specifications, are undoubtedly unjust. Marcel, whose whole philosophy could be summarized as the philosophy of a genuinely human experience, could not go along with that kind of uniform rationalistic universality, which so conveniently disregards the bumps that pave the real road to perfection. Without giving up the universal demands of human nature, he advised us to interpret them in the light of our Being insofar as the latter is always "in situation." He wrote:

> I would not like that the real meaning of these remarks were misconstrued by the reader. Of course, I am not advocating a return to the sadly narrow kind of rationalism that, regrettably, has constituted for forty years our official gospel. But Christian philosophy and Theology deserve undying glory, not only for not having ignored it for one moment, but also for having brought it up, instead, to its zenith, and grounded it in the indestructible foundations of Being. All it takes is to embody such a demand for universality in the most concrete modalities of human experience, without underestimating even one of them, but rather acknowledging that even the least one is susceptible of being deepened indefinitely if it is lived in full.48

Marcel's theater is full of cases in which one character
misjudges another because he or she ignores the real
motives of the latter. Such is the case with Claire in
regard to Roger, in Le Quattuor en fa dièze, and with
Abel Renaudier vis-a-vis his best friend Jacques Delorme
in L'Iconoclaste.[49] But not only is his Theater full of
value-judgments "in situation;" his experience itself
avails him with many a case in point. The chapter
titled In Search of Truth and Justice in his book
Searchings sheds plenty of light on the embodiment of
universality in experience that he was trying to put
forward in Homo Viator. He contrasts the fickleness of
a life lived according to moods with the consistency and
absolute stability that is called for by truth.
Emphasizing the aspect of universality, on the one hand,
he writes: "In any case, living according to
truth...means bringing ourselves into agreement with a
demand which has to express itself in us and cannot be
stifled."[50] Yet, on the other hand, bearing in mind the
changing demands imposed on the conscience by the
circumstances, he warns us: "This does not necessarily
mean that the demand must press forward into consciousness in entire universal character. Most probably it
will take shape when a particular situation demands it,
or when an action is required, regardless of the
personal risk involved."[51] Indeed, according to Marcel,
the flexibility of this conception of justice is not
another way of evading the rigors of the moral duty; the
tragic way in which the dictates of his conscience
turned out to be disastrous for a member of the French
Council of State under the Vichy regime does away with
all fear of moral laxity. As Marcel tells us: "During
Petains's trial he felt personally obliged to speak in

the marshal's behalf, whatever it might cost him personally...he was, if my memory serves me correctly, suspended for two years because he had testified in favor of a man whose fate had already been determined. Consequently, both he and his large family were forced to live under most difficult material conditions for the duration."52

John B. O'Malley is right when he reconciles both extreme demands in the notion of human person--or "essence-freedom," as we called it, and ultimately in the dynamic "pensée-pensante." "The moral is identified with the sterling human," he writes. And he goes on: "At the same time, the human ideal is recognised to be the fulfillment in being of the individual person. Within such a philosophic context, a phenomenological analysis of moral experience can develop at once existentially adequate and universally significant."53 The demands of human nature, therefore, cannot be viewed in a rationalistic way; they must be surprised, as it were, through the growing dynamism of the human person in the "situation" in which it is taking place. In this way, as O'Malley puts it, "conflicts between is and ought cease to be relevant, belonging as they do to argument that deals in objectively conceived propositions, problematically interpreted."54 They overlook entirely the simple declaration made by Marcel, to which his whole ethical thought reduces, namely, that "It is perhaps of my essence qua freedom to be able to conform or not to my essence qua nature."55 The ought must reach the person through the prism of her freedom or, to use once more O'Malley's enlightening formulas, "The is, indeed, is the affirmation of the person qua person in his total actuality which, in turn, embraces the ought of the existential exigency that declares his radical orientation towards ontological fulfillment."[56] All of these statements do, after all, come down to saying that being flung by our freedom in the direction of human perfection is as natural a phenomenon as having our body regenerate itself through nourishment. "It is indeed but the surfacing up on the level of the intelligence of the same mysterious activity that enables a tissue to make itself up again and an organ to undergo a process of regeneration"[57]--as Marcel himself puts it.

There is no doubt, therefore, that Marcel wages an all-out war in order to rescue what really counts, that is, the natural "_religio_," the strictly human values, and what he calls the "nuptial bond that links us to life," which is nothing more than the act by means of which life is accepted and developed in accordance with the noblest and deepest sense that ensues from a high consideration of our nature. From that point of view one can say that he advocates the formation at full steam of a unified front in which the Christians should condescend to motivate their moral exhortations on the basic level of their religion, leaving aside the strictly revealed data of the same, which may rather prove divisive. He is afraid that, as he puts it, many souls, having "yielded to the pressures of Jansenism have undoubtedly given in to the temptation of reneging the human and deserting the earth without thereby coming nevertheless too close to heaven. In turn,"--he adds-"I would be ready to believe that there is a _religio_ to which the very pagans bore a wonderful testimony through their piety towards their dead ones and their home deities, a piety which, on this side of Christian spirituality proper, guarantees the solidity of that contract between man and life to which I have referred many times in the past. It makes full sense, therefore, to expect that whenever such a piety yields to the merciless pressure which is applied, not by technology itself, to be sure, but by a mentality excessively imbued with fascination for technological achievements, the infractions to what our forefathers used to call the natural order should become more and more frequent, as is the case nowadays."58 Such a piety, he contends, would still be the salvation for our generation because it is "the only authentic vinculum capable of uniting all men among themselves on this side of Revelation." And it is so because it is the only recipe that is bound to translate universality into concreteness, so much so that, as Marcel warns us, "any abstract universalism that proclaims doing away with it, even if it is built on the best of intentions, will inexorably pave the way for a nihilism the devastating action of which is, as of now, beginning to be noticeable everywhere."59

Marcel was really frightened by such a prospect, which, in his mind, had us whirling down straight to the precipice of animality. This is why his ethical thought clung, as to the only possible salvation, to "rational" nature's noblest aspirations. Literally panic stricken, he complained: "Before my generation is gone, men will have witnessed a systematic subversion unravelling under their own eyes with an extraordinary tenacity and spreading its devastating power beyond the revealed datum and the sacred principles upheld by tradition until finally it reaches nature itself." Yet, reacting against his own depression, he dared to throw a cautious challenge: "No matter what some cheap biologists may think, man will never level with the animals: whenever he acts as himself and remains faithful to his vocation, he soars infinitely above them." "However," he warned, "whenever he deliberately reneges his mission, he falls infinitely below their level." In other words, he saw that the time of decision had come. Therefore, disowning any mediocre solution, he literally exploded in an outburst against the humanism promoted by those petty retiredVoltairians who called for a return to the golden mean, and thereby exalt the middle virtues as well as the smart calculations and the methodical precautions. With a touch of scorn he declared: "We now know for sure and through a tragic experience that such is but the galloping precursor of the worst national and personal disasters."60

It goes without saying that if this is the time of decision, human nature's demands must be taken in the fullness of their dogmatic force or else nothing will be achieved. Thus, leaving behind any relativism of the sort advocated by the Situation Ethics, he clearly warned us that "...we must recognize the trauma as a trauma and the anomaly as an anomaly; thereto, though," he added, "the notion of human order must be preserved despite the attacks that have long targeted it from all over."61 Then, furthering still more his survey of the unfinished business, he concluded: "what we must do above all is to restore a certain dogmatism whose foundations have been gradually undermined. Yet, a logical circle bars our way. For if its constitution is to be possible at all, it would seem that such a dogmatism needs as a foundation precisely the very conviction to which it is aimed. However," he went on, "the petitio principii is merely apparent. Indeed, it is true that if we propose it in purely intellectual terms, such a problem is unsolvable. But it so happens that any intellectual approach to it is totally inadequate." For, after all, he seems to be saying, this is a problem that arises among living beings and precisely because the latter are committed to a singular destiny which it is up to them to tackle and understand. On that level, therefore, we can draw the following inference: "perhaps we have enough foundation to assume that human beings can wake up to the awareness of Being in its plenitude if they realize the state of destruction and chaos to which any ontological nihilism necessarily leads."[62]

Certainly, the preservation of human nature could not have been placed any higher in Marcel's agenda. But, why?

5 - Human Nature as the Pointer to Divine Perfection.

If we inquire about that magic of human nature which forces Marcel to insist on absolute respect for what Kant calls "Humanity," we are bound to reach the peak of Marcel's Ethics. For in that endeavor human nature manifestsitself as leading directly to God insofar as it is the image of His Being and of His consistency and plenitude.[63] It is, we might say, a powerful reflector of the divine perfections, which cannot help but yoke our will to the divine imitation, thereby inciting it to transcend itself. In that sense, the consideration of human nature accounts for the essential restlessness of the human person that showed so vividly through Augustine's heart and consists in the fact that man

solely "becomes" to the extent that he tends to incarn-
ate in one work, in one action at a time, and finally in
the totality of his life, without however being able to
ever stiffen and crystallize in any particular incarnation. Why? Because, as Marcel puts it, "human nature
participates in the inexhaustible plenitude of the Being
from which it emanates. This is the reason why it is
impossible to think both the person and the personal
order without at the same time thinking what lies beyond
them, that is, a suprapersonal reality that presides
over all their initiatives and is, at the same time,
their origin and their end."[64] This amounts to
recognizing the distinction that the Scholastics had
already drawn between the constitutive proximate norm of
morality, human nature, and the ultimate one, the divine
Being. In other words, it is not our conception of God
that is based on the consideration of Man's Being,
rather it is man's perfections that are patterned after
God's nature. Hence the following deep remark to be
found in Homo Viator: "We find ourselves here on the
edge of a paradoxical truth in which the metaphysics of
the family is rooted: far from there being any reason to
think that it is theology that transposes rather arbitrarily some human relations to the sphere of the divine
realities, we must recognize instead that the presumably
natural relations--which, as we saw, can never be traced
to merely empirical data-- do not only symbolize some
transcendent relations towards which they steer our
fervor, but do also tend irresistibly to destroy and
dissolve themselves to the extent that the superior
matching relations are ignored and negated."[65] To put
it concretely, without the notion of God's paternity,
the real concept of human fatherhood would be
impossible.

But, by the same token, it is impossible to envisage human nature "adequately"--as we should if human nature is to be the constitutive norm of morality-- without including among its essential relations its very dependence on God. This, says Marcel, is most in view when we tackle the study of man's relation to the family: "The family"--he writes--"is the matrix in which the individuality is formed; as such it arises precisely at the very articulation between the vital and the spiritual orders." A penetrating remark ensues right away in his mind, which is worth pondering. "Furthermore," he adds, "the family is a real proof of the impossibility of separating one order from another. For it is only the purely speculative reason which may give the impression of their independence. Indeed, it plays for a stake, and proudly tries to forget the conditions of its own insertion in the world of real beings, thereby disregarding altogether the bonds that are inherent in the status of being a creature." At this point, Marcel engages in a remarkable meditation on createdness that we should listen to without interruption:

> And yet, ultimately it is on this
> notion of creature, which is both so
> elementary and so lavishly ignored,
> that the decisive accent must be
> placed. For it is a paradox worth
> paying attention to, that to the
> extent that man lets himself be
> carried away by a certain primary
> philosophy of science (not by
> science itself, mind you) and as a
> result winds up conceiving of

himself either as a mere link in an endless chain or as the product of merely natural forces, to that same extent he grants himself the right to behave as an absolute sovereign in regard to the regulation of his own life. That is to say that the more humiliated he finds himself de iure by a certain theoretical materialism which denies him any specific status as to his being and his activity, all the more grows in him a practical de facto pride that prompts him to deny the existence of any human order to which he should adjust himself.[66]

This passage is most enlightening. On the one hand, it shows a well balanced approach to technology. Contrary to what Kenneth T. Gallagher may fear,[67] it is not science that he is against; it is only a certain philosophical conception of the same. We even know that technology, as a fresh encounter with Being through invention, had all his blessings, it being only a blind, routine type of application of its discoveries that made him uneasy. He put it most clearly in Creative Fidelity, where he placed on the same level technological discovery and musical or poetical creations: "The same presence and the same appeal to the soul by the Being within it can be found in any creative act whether visible or not; the act, the same with itself despite the inexhaustibility of its manifestations, testifies to this same presence, and the soul can challenge or annul it insofar as it is a soul endowed with freedom."[68] On the other hand, we are told that his real point was that "indeed the human is not authentically human unless it is upheld by the incorruptible framework of the sacred."[69]

It is always the same junction between the spirit and life that comes to the surface. And Marcel falls literally into a state of ecstasy when he turns his attention to the wonderful cooperation between the flesh and the spirit that is called for by the nature of the conjugal act insofar as the latter is a human act rooted in the depths of our animality...It is in this combination that he finds the real meaning of marriage. "On the one hand"--he tells us--"it is manifest that the family, in its true essence, is incompatible with any matrimony which would be no more than an association based on either common interests or common tastes; marriage, indeed, is essentially ordained in some way to the idea of a posterity whose arrival is to be prepared. Yet, on the other hand, it should be equally emphasized as indubitable that, if contracted only in view of procreation, matrimony would be open to the risk of degenerating for lack of a solid spiritual base and would thereby constitute an attempt against the most venerable aspect of the specifically human order. For there is something insulting to the dignity of the human person if one of the partners views the spouse as a mere instrument of reproduction. If the carnal work is thus downgraded, chances are that a terrible revenge will brew and finally explode when the concealed and oppressed powers of the soul finally get rid of the yoke that was tyrannically imposed on them."[70] Undoubtedly, it is an affront to man because, by virtue of the power of taking a stand vis-à-vis its life, the human being has become far more than a mere living being, namely, a spirit.[71] This superiority, in turn, entails that man may eventually have to surrender his very right to bodily protection on the grounds of his moral responsibility towards society. In particular, going counter to today's myth that biolioicasl life is to be preserved above all, Marcel centers the problem of parenthood at the level of birth in the following balanced way: "Insofar as life is merely transmitted through the generating act"--he points out--"it is neither a benefit nor a malediction: it is only a possibility, an occasion, an opportunity, and as such it can be good or bad. But such a possibility can be realized only through a being which appears from the outset as a subject, i.e. as being able both to enjoy and mostly to suffer and also to become fully aware some day of what at first he had only experienced. Such a being, of course, should be fully equipped in such a way that, when he is able to take a stand in front of his life and appreciate it, the ambiguous original chance will appear to him as being actually a benefit. The parents have therefore the sacred obligation of behaving in such a way that someday the child will feel truly indebted to them."[72]

This constitutes the parents as God's cooperators in the highest possible creation. He writes in Searchings, "fatherhood is not biological; it has to do with a particular vocation. But this vocation itself presupposes a regard for life. It includes the corollary (of which we are perhaps all too unaware) that the words 'to impart life' have to be interpreted in their truest sense, namely, that life is an infinitely precious gift, and that the father himself is only a mediator between God as the author of all creation and

the child as a creature of God."73 In fact, this
conception makes the parents true creators. "The
meaning of the word creator"--he adds in Homo Viator--
"is here very precise. It points to the active collab-
oration that every free agent has the privilege to
contribute to the universal enterprise that is going on
in our world and, undoubtedly, infinitely beyond it."74
But the final convincing argument comes through the
following passage taken from Le vieux createur, in which
he draws the most important conclusion from this whole
conception of the family mystery:

> Negatively, such a vow or vocation
> means that our son does not belong
> to us any more than we belong to
> ourselves; furthermore, and more
> fundamentally, that he is not there
> even for himself and that
> consequently he should not be
> educated as though he ought to
> affirm some day that he depends only
> on himself. Indeed, it would be
> inconsistent on my part to allow him
> to have what I deny myself and to
> tolerate his becoming guilty someday
> of what I, for one, consider to be
> an infraction against the deep law
> of life. There is only one way out
> left, we must set as a principle
> that, just as ourselves, our
> children also are destined to a
> certain service by participating in
> an endeavor that as a whole we must
> humbly recognize as being beyond our

grasp, being all the more so as
regards its specific application to
the tender new will that we are
supposed to raise to the consciousness of itself.[75]

Marcel dramatized the ill consequences that are
bound to ensue when the child is raised as though he
were only a possession of the mother. A chain reaction
that makes other people unhappy is put in evidence in The
Votive Candle, where the obsession that Aline is going
through as a result of the death of her son Raymond at
the front makes her husband Octave break up their home,
and leads Raymond's fiancée, Mireille, to marry
Raymond's cousin in order to preserve Raymond's memory
intact as Aline had brainwashed her to do. Mireille,
who thus enters a life of sacrifice for a mere idea,
silences her love for Chanteuil and begins that life of
compassion for André. At the end of the play, though,
she explodes and blames Aline for having meddled in
their lives and for still doing so even then. "Now"--
she goes on in an outburst of rage--"what are you
trying to make me say? Now you're going to do as much
damage by your remorse as you did then by your tyranny.
Oh, I hate you! How I hate you."[76] But not only in
The Votive Candle does he make that point. In A Man of
God he sharply scolds Claude for the kind of virtuous
zeal that the latter displays in regard to his
daughter's well-being. Indeed, according to Marcel, he
loves her too much, but only "by the book." Unfortunately, he loves everybody in the same way, including his
wife: as though he were acting the role of a father, a
spouse, a son, but all along also the role of a pastor.
No wonder that at one point his wife, Edmée, vehemently

matches his rehearsed and hollow exclamation, "My darling, I am sharing my cross with you," with this whipping remark: "Claude, you are my husband, you are not a priest!"[77] But she shows him also, at another point, how far from being harmless his behavior is. She openly accuses him: "If you had really been my husband...I would never have been unfaithful to you."[78] His daughter, Osmonde, is perhaps more hurting and to the point. In her view he is such an unfit father precisely because he is guilty of not having ever been able to think of her as she really was; he always approached her as one of a family group, "living a humdrum existence in a happy Christian home, with texts on the wall and family prayers every morning."[79] Evidently, such a preparation for the kind of creator that Osmonde was called upon to be was a failure, and it was such a failure because it was altogether based on pure abstractions. Osmonde put it well: "I am always being told of self-denial and helping other people...Nothing has changed, nothing, I tell you, since the days when I was told to give my favorite doll to the orphans' home..."[80]

It is worth noting that Marcel is here consistently following the same line that he had embraced when he insisted on never construing the strict demands of human nature except "in situation." And, certainly, the motive is still the same: to keep his distance from the abstract rationalistic "codes" that literally were swarming when he began his reflections. By the same token, it was to be expected that he would apply his strict criteria even to the burning issues of abortion and divorce with the same rational flexibility and understanding. And so he did with a surprising freedom of mind.

For instance: he drew a very sensitive distinction between the particular acts of divorce, and the multiplication of the same. Indeed, he thought, whereas one particular divorce's circumstances may be in tune with the sacred meaning of the family institution, a rash of divorces undergone with very little reflection and out of fashion, can only show misconception of and even disregard for the sacred bond. He felt that whereas judgments bearing on particular events may be rash and unjustified, "the moral censure recovers its rights if it bears on social realities such as the proliferation of divorces or the generalization of birth control or even of the abortive practices. And certainly there will be room for an enlightened and fully justified condemnation if its target is an execrable campaign altogether directed at bestowing in principle a rational justification on such practices."81 The criterion is always the same: as long as the sacred bond with life is not clearly threatened--as is the case in certain situations in which the multiplicity of aspects may conceal a true demand for an exception precisely for the sake of the family institution--, caution is advisable. Marcel recognized it openly: "Besides," he said, "I am ready to grant that in this realm it is difficult and even impossible to draw a clear-cut dividing line between what is allowed and what is not. There are indeed situations where it is impossible to pass judgment knowing fully well what we are doing if a detailed examination of each case and of the principles that are involved in it has not successively preceded. Yet, we can affirm without any doubt--and this is what really counts from my point of view-- that all distinctions disappear and that man digs an irreparable breach through which what is monstrous gains access as soon as the piety towards life crumbles in him. Because the latter is what alone can orient his initiatives in that order where homicide looms so easy, so indiscernible, so enticing, that at times it cannot even be held as homicide by the one that carries it out."82

Marcel was right, therefore, when he stretched our views on the nuptial bond with life to the infinite horizons of the light of Christ as we saw him doing in a previous chapter. For his emphasis on the need to found the community on the demands of human nature precisely as the latter show up in the splendor that humanity acquires in the Divine Word was the best immunization against the blurring effect of the sensible world. A sign that this belongs still to his Natural Ethics is that he did it while remaining all along on this side of the Divine Revelation.

footnotes

1MB, II, p. 126.

2Karl Jaspers, Introduction to Philosophy (Zurich, 1949). Cited by Marcel in MB, II, p. 127. St. Thomas agrees:"...homo est liberi arbitrii, alioquin frustra essent consilia, exhortationes praecepta, prohibit5iones, praemia et poenae." See S.Th., I, q.83,a.1, in c.

3MB, II, pp. 123-124. Aquinas echoes this view. See S.Th., I,q.83, a.1, ad 5m.

4I,c,, p. 123.

5See St. Thomas, S.Th., 1-2,q.1,a.6, in c.

6Malebranche, Traité de la nature et de la grâce. Cited by Aimé Forest, Consentement et Création (Paris: Aubier, 1943), p. 44.

7MB, II, pp. 128-129.

80.c., p. 125.

9Ibid.

10BH, p. 110. See also PhEx, p. 24.

110.c., pp. 106-107.

12CrF, p. 65.

13PhEx, pp. 81-82.

14MB, II, p. 105.

[15]Michele Federico Sciacca, La libertà e il tempo [LT] (Milan: Marzorati, editore, 1965), p. 83.

[16]Michele Federico Sciacca, Ontologia Triadica e Trinitaria [OTT] (Milan: Marzorati, editore, 1972), pp. 62-63.

[17]LT, p. 83.

[18]Xavier Zubiri, Naturaleza, Historia, Dios (Madrid, 1944), p. 457. Zubiri further links pride with atheism. He writes: "Any existence which does not feel ligated is an atheist existence, an existence that has not reached yet its ontological foundation. Now such lack of awareness goes hand in hand with the person's self-sufficiency as far as the success of the earthly life is concerned...Only a first class spirit can keep the sense of religation in the midst of the complicated success of its vital process." (O.c., p. 461).

[19]CrF, p. 167.

[20]O.c., p. 46.

[21]PhEx, pp. 82-83.

[22]Ibid.

[23]Jean-Paul Sartre, Critique de la raison dialectique (Paris: Gallimard, 1960), p. 248.

[24]MB, II, p. 131.

[25]MB, II, p. 130.

[26]MB, II, pp. 106-107.

[27]PhEx, p. 48.

[28]O.c., p. 87.

[29]Marcel, L'homme problématique [HP], 1955., p. 58.

[30]HP, p. 38.

[31]Ibid.

[32]O.c., p. 40.

[33]Ibid.

[34]Ibid.

[35]Ibid.

[36]O.c., p. 41.

[37]O.c., p. 49.

[38]HV, pp. 219-220. See also on p. 158 how he repudiates that same pessimism in both Heidegger's and Sartre's philosophical thoughts. See Neil Gillman, Gabriel Marcel On Religious Knowledge (Washington, D.C.: University Press of America, 1980), pp. 185-190.

[39]HV, p. 219.

[40]O.c., p. 97.

[41]HP, p. 21.

[42]See BH, pp. 106-107.

[43]HV, p. 29.

[44]HP, p. 21.

[45]PhEx, p. 58.

[46]HV, p. 31.

[47]HV, pp. 33-34.

[48]HV, p. 34. This text seems to belie the mistrust of at least Thomism that Seymour Cain attributes to Marcel in his Gabriel Marcel (South Bend, Indiana: Regnery/Gateway, Inc.)

[49]See Marcel's report in The Existential Background of Human Dignity, pp. 48-52.

[50]Searchings, p. 16.

[51]Ibid.

[52]O.c., pp. 16-17.

[53]John B. O'Malley, The Fellowship of Being (The Hague: Martinus Nijhoff, 1966), p. 136.

[54]Ibid.

[55]MB, II, pp. 106-107.

[56]Ibid.

[57]HV, p. 227.

[58]HV, p. 127.

[59]HV, pp. 225-227.

[60]HV, p. 127.

[61]HV, pp. 292-293.

[62]Ibid.

[63]HV, p. 281.

[64]HV, pp. 32-33.

[65]HV, p. 131.

[66]HV, pp. 130-131.

[67]See Gallagher, Kenneth T., The Philosophy of Gabriel Marcel (New York: Fordham University Press, 1966), pp. 147-157.

[68]CrF, p. 10; see Peccorini, Gabriel Marcel: La "Razón de Ser" en la "Participación", pp. 267-270, footnote #154;PhEx, p. 31, BH, pp. 125-128; MAMAS, pp. 91-92.

[69]HV, p. 132. See also Le Chemin de Crète (Paris: Bernard Grapet, 1936), pp. 137-139 and 167.

[70]HV, p. 120.

[71]See HV, p. 116.

[72]HV, p. 125.

[73]Searchings, p. 48.

[74]HV, p. 121.

[75]HV, pp. 165-166.

[76]Gabriel Marcel Three Plays [GM3Plays], 1965, pp. 277-278.

[77]GM3Plays, p. 65.

[78]O.c., pp. 78-79.

[79]

[80]O.c., p. 89.

[81]HV, p. 122.

[82]HV, p. 228.

Select Bibliography

Marcel's works quoted and their abbreviated references

1912   "Les conditions dialectiques de la Philosophie de l'Intuition," in Revue de Métaphysique et de Morale, 9(1912) [CDPI]

1927   Journal Métaphysique (Paris: Gallimard, 1927) [JM]

1935   Être et Avoir (Paris: Aubier, 1935) [EA]

1945   Du refus à l'invocation (Paris:Aubier, 1945) [HV]

       La métaphysique de Royce (Paris:Aubier, 1945) [MR]

1949   Position et approches concrètes du mystère ontologique. Introduction par Marcel de Corte (Louvain: Nauwelaerts, 1949) [PACMO]

1951   Les hommes contre l'humain (Paris:Aubier, 1951) [HCH]

       Le Mystère de l'être .Vol.I: Reflection et Mystère Vol.II: Foi et réalité (Paris:Aubier, 1951) [ME,I or II]

       Homo Viator, Trans. Emma Craufurd (Chicago:Regnery) [HV]

1952   Metaphysical Journal. Trans. Bernard Wall (Chicago:Regnery, 1951) [MJ]

1955   L'homme problèmatique (Paris:Aubier, 1955) [HP]

1956   Tdhe Philosophy of Existentialism. Trans.
        Manya Harari (New York:The Citadel Press,
        1956) [Ph.Ex.]

1959   Présence et immortalité (Paris:Flammarion,
        1959) [PI]

1961   Fragments philosophiques 1909-1914
        (Louvain:Nauwelaerts, 1961) [FrPh]

1962   Man Against Mass Society. Trans. G.S.
        Fraser (Chicago:Regnery, 1952 and 1962)
        [MAMS]

        (There was another edition published in
        England with a different title: Man Against
        Humanity. Trans. G.S. Fraser
        (London: HarvillPress 1952)

1963   The Existential Background of Human
        Existence. The William James Lectures (Cam-
        bridge, Massachusetts: Harvard University
        Press, 1963). [EBHE]

1964   La dignité humaine et ses assises
        existentielles (Paris:Aubier, 1964) [DHAE]

        The Mystery of Being. 1. Reflection and
        Mystery 2. Faith and Reality (Chicago:A
        Gateway Edition, 1964) [MB]

1965   Being and Having. An Existential Diary
        Presented by James Collins, trans. by
        Katherine Farrer (New York: Harper and Row,
        1965) [BH]

        Gabriel Marcel Three Plays. A Man of God,
        Ariadne, The Votive Candle. Introduction by
        Richard Hayes, trans. by Rosalind Haywood
        and Marjorie Gabain (New York: Hill and
        Wang, 1965) [GM3Plays]

Paix sur la terre (Paris: Aubier, 1965) [PT]

Philosophical Fragments 1909-1914 and The
Philosopher and Peace. Trans. Lionel A.
Blain (Notre Dame:University of Notre Dame
Press, 1965) [PhFr]

1967   Searchings (New York:Newman Press;Toronto:
Glen Rock, 1967) [Searchings]

1968   Entretiens Paul Ricoeur-Gabriel Marcel
(Paris:Aubier, 1968) [ERGB]

Pour une sagesse tragique et son au'delà
(Paris:Librairie Plon, 1968) [PSTr.]

1971   En chemin vers quel éveil?
(Paris:Gallimard, 1971) [EChE]

1973   Tragic Wisdom and Beyond. It includes
conversations between Paul Ricoeur and
Gabriel Marcel. Trans. by Stephen Jolin and
Peter McCormick (Evanston:Northwestern
University, 1973) [TrW]

1974   Creative Fidelity. English Translation of
Du Refus à l'invocation by Robert Rosthal
(New York:TheNoonday Press, a Division of
Farrar, Straus and Girous, 1974) [CrF]

"Dialogues entre G. Marcel et Mme. Parain-
Vial" [See: "Extraits des entretiens qui
eurent lieu à Dijon les 17 et 18 mars 1973
sur la pensée de Gabriel Marcel," in Revue
de Métaphysique et de Morale, 79 (1974), pp.
383-392]

1976   Entretiens autour de Gabrie Marcel (Langages
à la Baconière, Neuchâtel, 1976

1977   Gabriel Marcel interrogé par Pierre Boutang.
Suivi de Position et approches concrètes du
mystère ontologique. Jean Michel Place,

editeur (Publié avec le concours de la
Fohdation Européenne de la culture par
"Présence de Gabriel Marcel," 1977)

1979   "Gabriel Marcel et la pensée allemande.
Nietsche, Heidegger, Ernst Bloch," in
Présence de Gabriel Marcel, Cahier I
(Aubier, 1979)

Cain, Seymour, <u>Gabriel</u> <u>Marcel</u> (South Bend, Indiana:Regency/Gateway, Inc., 1979).

Cheetham, M. "L'actualité du `Monde Cassé' de G. Marcel" [See: "Extraits des Entretiens qui eurent lieu à Dijon les 17 et 18 mars 1973 sur la pensée de Gabriel Marcel," in <u>Revue</u> <u>de</u> <u>Metáphysique</u> <u>et</u> <u>de</u> <u>Morale</u>, 79 (1974), pp. 367-370.]

Delhomme, Jeanne, "Le jugement en `je'," in <u>Revue</u> <u>de</u> <u>Métaphysique</u> <u>et</u> <u>de</u> <u>Morale</u>, 79(1974), pp. 289-370.

Gallagher, Kenneth T, <u>The</u> <u>Philosophy</u> <u>of</u> <u>Gabriel</u> <u>Marcel</u> (New York:Fordham University Press, 1966).

Gillman, Neil, <u>Gabriel</u> <u>Marcel</u> <u>On</u> <u>Religious</u> <u>Knowledge</u> (Washington, D.C.:University Press of America, 1980).

O'Malley, John B., <u>The</u> <u>Fellowship</u> <u>of</u> <u>Being</u> (The Hague:Martinus Nijhoff, 1966).

Parain-Vial, Jeanne, <u>Gabriel</u> <u>Marcel</u> <u>et</u> <u>les</u> <u>niveaux</u> <u>de</u> <u>l'expérience</u> (Paris: Pierre Schers, editeur, 1966)

Troisfontaines, Roger, (a) <u>De</u> <u>l'Existence</u> <u>à</u> <u>l'Être</u> (Louvain:Nauwelaerts, 1953 and 1968).
               (b) "Les mystéres de la mort" (see "Extraits des entretiens qui eurent lieu à Dijon..."), in <u>Revue</u> <u>de</u> <u>Métaphysique</u> <u>et</u> <u>de</u> <u>Morale</u>, 79(1974) pp. 328-343.

Index of Names

Aquinas: 8, 51, 94,133.
Aristotle: 8, 9, 23, 24, 25, 26, 27, 28, 31, 32-33, 34, 41, 57, 92, 93-94.
Augustine: 122, 166.

Berger, Pierre: 87, 88, 89.
Bergson, Henri: 18, 20, 36.
Bernard of Clairvaux: 133.
Berning, Vincent: 15, 16.
Binswanger: 107.
Blain, Lionel: 35.
Blondel, Maurice: 31, 35, 141.
Bollnow, C.F.: 16.
Boutang, Pierre: 9, 92, 93, 105.
Brunchswicg, Léon: 4, 17, 105.
Buber, Martin: 15.

Cain, Seymour: 6, 7, 8, 9.

Delhomme, Jeanne: 51, 52.
Descartes, René: 92, 95, 146, 158.

Eckhard, Master: 44.

Gallagher, Kenneth T.: 169.
Grean, Stanley: Acknowledgments
Grotius: 8.

Heidegger, Martin: 13, 15, 77, 99, 106, 107, 108, 109, 110, 111, 146, 147.
Horvath, Tibor: Acknowledgments
Husserl, Edmund: 6.

John the Evangelist: 89, 90, 96.

Kant, Immanuel: 37, 38, 40, 45, 52, 54, 120, 141, 147, 166.

Lavelle, Louis: 35.
Locke, John: 56.

PROBLEMS IN CONTEMPORARY PHILOSOPHY